BIBLICAL ARCHAEOLOGY

Documents from the British Museum

BIBLICAL ARCHAEOLOGY

Documents from the British Museum

T.C. MITCHELL

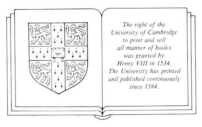

The right of the
University of Cambridge
to print and sell
all manner of books
was granted by
Henry VIII in 1534.
The University has printed
and published continuously
since 1584.

CAMBRIDGE UNIVERSITY PRESS

Cambridge

New York   New Rochelle   Melbourne   Sydney

Published in North America by the Press Syndicate of the
University of Cambridge
32 East 57th Street, New York, New York 10022

First published 1988

Library of Congress Cataloging-in-Publication Data

Mitchell, T.C.
  Biblical archaeology: documents from the British Museum / T.C.
Mitchell.
    p. cm.
  ISBN 0-521-36323-3.   ISBN 0-52-36867-7 (pbk.)
  1. Bible—Antiquities.   2. British Museum—Catalogs.   I. British
Museum.   II. Title.
BS621.M56 1988   88-9592
220.9′3—dc19   CIP

Set in 11 on 11½pt Bembo
Printed and bound in Great Britain

Designed by Adrian Hodgkins
  Cover: Chris Millett

Cover: Israelite captives leaving the city of Lachish
after its capture by Sennacherib in 701 BC.
See page 60.

Contents

Preface

When the student of the ancient Near East begins to look at the text of the Bible in detail he finds that it betrays itself as a product of that world. This is largely masked in the Authorised Version, whose translators worked before the great archaeological discoveries of the nineteenth century. In their hands the text became such a monument of English literature that it took on a quite different character, a character which has been carried over into many more recent translations. One of the things I have tried to bring out in this book, therefore, is the Near Eastern character of the Bible, and this has inevitably meant that it has been necessary to go into what may seem like inordinate detail in certain instances. It is intended however that a broad impression will emerge, while the simplified chronological charts which are included will set the material discussed within its historical context.

In the Further Reading I have aimed to give enough guidance for the layman to follow up the details, and also the opportunity to enter this fascinating field of study in more depth.

I have received advice and information from a number of colleagues in the Museum and the British Library, not all of which I have followed precisely, so in naming them I am not associating them with the result: Carol Andrews, Morris Bierbrier, Brian Cook, John Curtis, Antony Griffiths, Tom Pattie, Timothy Potter, Dr. D. Rowland-Smith, Veronica Tatton-Brown, Jonathan Tubb, Christopher Walker and Susan Walker.

I am grateful to the Keepers of other Departments in the Museum and in the British Library for allowing me to make use of photographs of objects in their care. The abbreviations appearing in the captions to the illustrations indicate their Departments of origin as follows: BL = British Library, E = Egyptian Antiquities, GR = Greek and Roman Antiquities, PD = Prints and Drawings, and WAA = Western Asiatic Antiquities.

In addition I would like in particular to thank Ann Searight for preparing the bulk of the artwork with her usual speed and accuracy, Irving Finkel for copying the cuneiform extracts with such an elegant hand, Bernadette Heaney for typing out the text and playing a large part in the preparation of the index, Barbara Winter for taking a number of the photographs, and Suzannah Gough of BMP for the time and trouble she has devoted to this modest volume.

T. C. MITCHELL

Introduction

BIBLICAL ARCHAEOLOGY

The word 'archaeology' was used by the ancient Greeks (spelt *archaiologia*) to mean ancient legend, or antiquarian tradition, and was first recorded in English in 1607, when Bishop Joseph Hall referred to 'all the archaiology of the Jewes till Saul's gouernment'. Since at that time the only knowledge of ancient Israel came from such written sources as the Bible, Bishop Hall was clearly using the word in this limited sense, and was not referring to objects dug out of the ground, or even ancient ruins still visible above ground. This latter sense only came into use during the early nineteenth century, when the word was spelt 'archaeology' and referred to the study of prehistoric monuments and excavated remains independent of written records. This meaning held sway for some time, but with the rediscovery by excavation of the ancient literate civilisations, it became plain that inscriptions were so inextricably associated with objects, that the archaeology of an area such as Mesopotamia had to embrace all aspects of the study, including the contents of the cuneiform inscriptions. Today the term 'archaeology' can be used very widely to embrace the study of the remains, including inscriptions where available, of all areas from prehistoric to modern times.

In view of the great flexibility in the use of this term, it is as well to make clear what its scope will be in this book. While its geographical and chronological limits will be defined by the word 'Biblical', shortly to be discussed, 'archaeology' will be taken here to include inscriptions, and will be extended to include manuscripts of later date than the time covered, the relevance of which will be set out below.

If 'archaeology' is so all-embracing, how much of it does 'Biblical' include? There is in this some variation in usage. Some would confine it largely to Palestine and others would include the whole world of the Bible, as for instance was assumed in 1870 when a 'Society of Biblical Archaeology' was founded in London, the main aims of which were 'the investigation of the Archaeology, Chronology, Geography and History of Ancient and Modern Assyria, Arabia, Palestine and other Biblical lands, [and] the promotion of the study of the Antiquities of those countries'. This interpretation will be adopted here, following in a British Museum tradition, since a leading figure in the foundation of the Society was Dr. Samuel Birch, the Keeper of the Department of Oriental (subsequently Egyptian and Assyrian) Antiquities in the British Museum from 1860–85.

Since the events narrated in the Bible cover the period from early times until the first century AD, and took place not only in Western Asia and Egypt, but also in Greece and Italy, the archaeological remains of all these periods and areas may be seen as legitimate material for the study of the Biblical Archaeologist.

During the eighteenth century, knowledge of the world of the Bible depended entirely on the Bible itself and such other written sources as the *Antiquities of the Jews* by Josephus. When students read the description in Jeremiah 18:1–12 of the potter at work (see Document **36**) they had no idea what the pot would have looked liked. The Biblical subjects so frequently undertaken by painters depicted men and women in clothing and with buildings and objects of everyday life which were those known to the artist in his time, with whatever oriental flavour could be given to them in the light of knowledge of the Ottoman Empire, or of accounts of the Arab world brought back by travellers. The etching in Figure 1, for instance, made by Rembrandt in the seventeenth century, which shows Abraham expelling Hagar and Ishmael from his house while Sarah and Isaac remain, depicts Abraham in a vaguely oriental turban and non-descript robes.

Fig 1
Etching by Rembrandt,
1637, showing Abraham
casting out Hagar and
Ishmael. P&D 1847-6-9-14

    This was the state of knowledge when the British Museum was first opened to
the public in 1759, though it was only two years later, in 1761, that there set out from
Copenhagen an expedition sponsored by the Danish King bound for the near east.
The sole survivor of this expedition, Carsten Niebuhr, recorded what he saw with
such admirable accuracy that his copies of cuneiform inscriptions on the monuments
at Persepolis, published in 1778, formed the basis of much of the early work on
decipherment. This decipherment took some years to accomplish, but his illustrations
of the relief sculptures at Persepolis gave Europeans a glimpse of the dress and equipment

of ancient orientals. Illustrations of Egyptian monuments and antiquities had only become available in Europe shortly before this, from about the middle of the eighteenth century.

The second half of the eighteenth century saw an increasing academic study of the Bible in a number of pioneering works in Biblical criticism – Astruc (1753), Michaelis (1770–75), Eichhorn (1780), Geddes (1792) and Ilgen (1798) on the Old Testament; and Michaelis (1750) and Reimarus through Lessing (1774–8) on the New Testament – but this was almost entirely armchair work. That is to say, they examined the Biblical books and then speculated freely in virtual isolation.

There was a veritable revolution in knowledge of the Biblical World during the nineteenth century. Already in 1802 Grotefend succeeded in reading some proper names in the Old Persian inscriptions published by Niebuhr, and in the same year Åkerblad and de Sacy fixed the value of some of the Demotic characters on the Rosetta stone (see Document **47**) which had been discovered in 1799 and was first displayed in the British Museum in 1802.

In 1808 Claudius James Rich arrived in Baghdad as a British Resident. His *Memoir on the Ruins of Babylon* (1815) revealed the possibilities of investigation on the ground and was a catalyst for further fieldwork. And so followed Champollion's publication of his decipherment of Egyptian Hieroglyphics in 1822 (see Document **47**), Rawlinson's publication of his decipherments of the Old Persian and Babylonian versions of the Behistun inscription in 1846 and 1851 respectively (see Document **45**), Botta's excavations at Nineveh and Khorsabad between 1842 and 1855, and those of Layard at Nineveh, Numrud, Ashur, Babylon and other sites between 1845 and 1851, and the recordings, explorations and excavations in Egypt of Champollion in 1828 and 1829, Lepsius between 1842 and 1845, Mariette between 1850 and 1881 and, in a somewhat different category, Belzoni between 1816 and 1820.

The discoveries made during these years and published in large folio volumes by Champollion (1809–28), Botta (1849–50), Layard (1849–53) and Lepsius (1849–59) provided a wealth of material about the costume, equipment and setting of the ancient Assyrians and Egyptians, and the texts now being newly translated gave the names of rulers, cities and countries. In his address in 1870 to the newly formed Society of Biblical Achaeology Dr Samuel Birch was able to identify the Hebrew kings Omri, Ahab, Jehu, Azariah (but see Document **31**), Menahem, Pekah, Hoshea, Hezekiah and Manasseh, the Assyrian kings Tiglath-Pileser I and II [now III], Sargon, Sennacherib, Esarhaddon and Ashurbanipal, the Egyptian Tirhaka, and the Syrians Benhadad, Hazael and Rezin. This shows the rapid progress of philological study in the decades following decipherment, but it is interesting to note that having dealt with Egypt and Mesopotamia, as well as Phoenicia and Sinai, he details other areas from which interesting and important material is to be expected, and continues, 'One of these is Palestine, whence it is much to be regretted so few, if any, monuments have been obtained which can be referred to the days of the Jewish monarchy – most of those discovered having inscriptions which do not date anterior to the Roman Empire'. He goes on, however, to mention the Moabite Stone (Document **18**) which had been discovered two years before, and what is now called the Royal Steward Inscription (Document **25**) only recently discovered at that time, but these monuments were quite in isolation.

Though some ill understood soundings had been made at Jerusalem by Lieutenants Charles Wilson (1864–5) and Charles Warren (1867–8), — the latter under the aegis of the Palestine Exploration Fund which had been founded in 1865 — no serious excavation was undertaken in Palestine until W.M. Flinders Petrie began work at the mound of Tell el-Hesy in 1890. He spent only six weeks on the site, but his work

set in motion the process which has led to the accumulation of an immense body of data on the archaeology of Palestine. It is worth noting however that progress was slow in the early years, and that for instance in 1908 Professor S.R. Driver in his lectures 'Modern Research as illustrating the Bible', could only report on excavations at eight sites, namely Tell el-Hesy, Gezer, Taanach, Megiddo, Tell es-Safi, Tell Zakariya, Tell ej-Judeideh, and Tell Sandahannah, only the first four of which could be called really substantial. The extent of knowledge still to be recovered is illustrated by his statement that 'The excavations show no trace of a break between the Canaanite and Israelite culture: there is no sudden change from one to the other; the transition is gradual'. While it is true that the Israelites adopted much of the material culture of their predecessors, it is now clear that there was a violent break at several sites.

The period between the two World Wars saw a healthy increase in the number of excavations in Palestine, and this trend has been greatly expanded over the last forty years, so that there is now a wealth of material for the reconstruction of the culture of ancient Palestine and indeed the sequence of pottery types is now better known than in any other area of the Near East.

The period since the end of the First World War has in fact been a time of extensive excavation throughout the Bible Lands, and a great deal of information is available not only on the general ancient history of the area, but also on specific details.

Mention has already been made of the fact that most of the early excavators had a lively awareness of the bearing their discoveries had on the Bible. Among those on the staff of the British Museum, Samuel Birch has already been referred to, and many of his successors have manifested a similar interest. George Smith, perhaps best known of early workers in the field, in describing the development of his interest in eastern explorations and discoveries explains that 'in 1866, seeing the unsatisfactory state of our knowledge of those parts of Assyrian history which bore upon the history of the Bible, I felt anxious to do something towards settling a few of the questions involved.' He joined the staff of the Museum in 1867 and many of his early publications dealt with the Assyrian royal inscriptions, in which he took due note of references to Israel and Judah. Many of the results referred to by Birch in his 1870 lecture derived from the work of Smith. The trend of Smith's interests are clear from the titles of two of his books, *The Assyrian Eponym Canon; Containing Translations of the Documents, and an Account of the Evidence, on The Comparative Chronology of the Assyrian and Jewish Kingdoms, from the Death of Solomon to Nebuchadnezzar* (1875), and *The Chaldaean Account of Genesis Containing the Description of the Creation, the Fall of Man, the Deluge, the Tower of Babel, the Times of the Patriarchs, and Nimrod; Babylonian Fables, and Legends of the Gods; from the Cuneiform Inscriptions* (1876). Following in the same tradition E.A. Wallis Budge, Keeper of Egyptian and Assyrian Antiquities, cooperated with Sir Edward Maunde Thompson, Principal Librarian of the Museum, in 1900 to prepare an appendix to the Oxford University Press *Helps to the Study of the Bible*, entitled 'Bible Illustrations' which illustrated and described 124 antiquities and manuscripts in this category. A revised version of this, edited by H.R.H. Hall, S. Smith and S.R.K. Glanville, the Keeper and Assistant Keepers respectively of Egyptian and Assyrian Antiquities appeared in 1931. Very well known to a later generation has been the volume *Archaeology and the Bible* (1940) by Sir Frederick Kenyon, and in more recent years D.J. Wiseman's *Illustrations from Biblical Archaeology* (1958) and R.D. Barnett's *Illustrations of Old Testament History* (1966, rev. ed. 1977) have kept up the tradition. Inevitably the present monograph includes many of the items dealt with in these earlier publications, because their relevance to Biblical studies continues.

The British Museum was established in 1753 to take charge of the library and collections of Sir Hans Sloane (1660–1753) and for the next 220 years manuscripts and books formed part of the Museum collections. When in 1933 the Codex Sinaiticus was purchased from the Russian authorities, it was the Museum which carried out the transaction.

In 1973 a division was made according to which the Department of Printed Books together with those of Manuscripts and of Oriental Manuscripts and Printed Books, became a separate institution, the British Library. This means that many manuscripts formerly described as part of the British Museum collections are now part of the collections of the British Library (in this volume, Documents **48, 54, 55, 59, 60**). They are distinguished by a prefixed BL.

ANCIENT TEXTS

It is inevitable that a large proportion of the antiquities which have a notable bearing on the Bible are written records because personal and geographical names are found in them as well as literary forms, grammatical constructions and vocabulary words which can all be compared.

Hundreds of thousands of ancient texts have been discovered in Mesopotamia, and Egypt, thousands in Iran, Asia Minor, Syria and South Arabia and hundreds in Palestine. They were inscribed on a variety of materials, especially clay in Mesopotamia, Syria and Asia Minor, and on papyrus in Egypt.

The texts themselves range from simple economic records (e.g. lists of rations issued), to letters, records of law cases, accounts of public works and military campaigns, law codes and treaties, to literary compositions of the imagination.

The scripts employed fall into three main types: pictographic (hieroglyphic), cuneiform and alphabetic. The 'hieroglyphic' script was used chiefly in Egypt where the more cursive Hieratic and Demotic forms developed alongside it in the later periods. The cuneiform script, so-called from being written with characters made up of wedge-shaped (Latin *cuneus*) lines, was invented in Mesopotamia, the area of Babylonia and Assyria, where it continued to be used into the first century of the Christian era, and was adopted in Iran, Syria and Asia Minor. All of these areas employed it in the form of a syllabary together with word-signs, but as a method of writing on clay or stone it was adapted at Ugarit in Syria to a purely alphabetic use, and in the Achaemenian Empire it was used in a very much simplified syllabary to write the imperial language today called Old Persian (see Document **45**). Egyptian hieroglyphs and cuneiform were invented around 3000 BC but the alphabetic script (see Document **6**) did not appear until after 2000 BC, and eventually superseded them and became the vehicle of many ancient languages.

One script can be used to write more than one language, and a language can be written in more than one script, so in describing a text it is usually necessary to specify the script and the language. The Egyptian scripts normally convey texts in the Egyptian language which changed gradually over the centuries. Cuneiform was used for Sumerian, Akkadian (which developed into the Babylonian and Assyrian dialects), Elamite, Hittite, and several other languages. The linear alphabet which appears first to have been used to write a west Semitic language (Document **5**) developed in the late second and early first millennia BC as the script of the Phoenicians which branched subsequently to Hebrew (Documents **6, 22, 25, 37–39, 41**) and Aramaic (Documents **30, 46**) and such rather meagrely represented languages as Ammonite, Moabite (Documents **18, 34**) and Edomite.

The Phoenicians, who were in fact first millenium BC coastal Canaanites, developed widespread trade throughout the Mediterranean with numerous colonies, of which the best known was Carthage. It was through them that the alphabet was passed to the Greeks (Documents **47, 48, 54-59**) and via the Etruscans to the Romans from whom we received our own alphabet. The Aramaeans were prominent in north Syria in the first millennium BC and were settled throughout Mesopotamia.

One of the things which excited the nineteenth-century decipherers, as has already been mentioned, was the discovery that not only were the names of Egyptian, Assyrian, Babylonian and Persian rulers, some of them long familiar from the Bible, found in recognisable form in the hieroglyphic and cuneiform texts, but also that the names of some of the kings of Israel and Judah appeared in them. These individuals were not always recognised at first. When Rawlinson published a translation of the text on the Black Obelisk of Shalmaneser III, one of the best known monuments of Biblical Archaeology (Document **16**), he read the name of the tributary, now known to have been Jehu, as 'Yahua son of Hubiri' and wrote that he was 'a prince of whom there is no mention in the annals and of whose native country therefore I am ignorant'.

The inscriptions also mentioned many place-names known from the Bible. These were not only in the great centres of civilisation – the Calah of Genesis 10:11 for instance being readily recognisable as Kalhu (modern Nimrud), one of the capitals of ancient Assyria – but also in Palestine itself (see Documents **7, 8, 9, 18, 22, 26, 27, 31**).

The cuneiform script, in the periods with which this book is concerned, made use of phonetic syllabic signs and logograms (word signs), but also, as aids to understanding, determinatives and phonetic complements which were not pronounced. Certain conventions have become accepted for representing these cuneiform signs in romanised script in such a way that the original signs can be restored from the transliteration.

(a) Syllabic signs. Since not only can a single sign have more that one phonetic value (polyphony of signs), but also several different signs can have the same phonetic value (homophony of signs) homophonous phonetic values are distinguished by numbers. Thus the phonetic value 'ba' can be written *ba, bá, bà, ba₄, ba₅* and so forth, each instance representing a different cuneiform sign. The values *bá* and *bà* simply represent *ba₂* and *ba₃* in an economical way, and no accentuation or special pronunciation is implied by the accents.

A few diacritical marks are used in the transliteration of the Semitic languages to represent sounds for which the Roman alphabet does not have individual characters:

> ’ = smooth breathing or glottal stop; as between i and a in 'I am'.
>
> ‘ = rough breathing, not used in English.
>
> ḥ = rough h, as in lo*ch*
>
> ḫ = hard h, as in lo*ch* more harshly pronounced.
>
> š = sh
>
> q = emphatic k
>
> ṣ = emphatic s
>
> ṭ = emphatic t

(b) Logograms. The words represented by these signs are transliterated in the grammatical forms appropriate to their contexts, an indication of which is often given by the plural sign (c) or a phonetic complement (d).

(c) Determinatives. A number of logograms serve in some contexts as determinative signs, usually written before the determined word. In transliteration these are sometimes represented by the Sumerian value written in capital letters, e.g. URU *as-tar-tu* (Document **19**), but in this book the alternative will be used of writing the Akkadian equivalent above the line, eg. ^{ālu}*as-tar-tu*. In a few instances modern abbreviations, e.g. ^d for ^{ilu} will also be used.

The determinatives appearing in this book are:

Before words
> d = ilu = DINGIR = god's name
>
> m = male name
>
> amēlu = LÚ = people
>
> ālu = URU = city
>
> mātu = KUR = country, land
>
> iṣu = GIŠ = wood

After words
> ki = ašru = KI = place
>
> pl. = MEŠ = plural.

(d) Phonetic Complements. When a logogram could have more than one possible reading a phonetic sign following it would indicate the correct one; e.g. *i-na qāti(ti)-šu* 'in his hand' (Document **8**) which shows that *qāti* and not *qātu* is the correct reading. Phonetic complements will be shown in parentheses following the complemented word, on the same line.

Egyptologists normally represent the glottal stop (the equivalent of Semitic 'aleph) by the symbol 3, but for simplicity and consistency, this value will here be represent by '. Classical scholars normally transliterate the Greek vowel *u* (*upsilon*) by the semivowel *y*, but since elsewhere in this book *y* is always used to represent a consonant, *upsilon* will here be transliterated *u*, to avoid confusion.

THE BIBLICAL WORLD

The Bible, which from Genesis chapter 11 onwards contains a history of the Hebrew people from about 2000 BC to the first century AD, begins with glimpses of the preceding history of mankind, notably the Creation, the Flood, and the episode of the Tower of Babel. The contents of Genesis 1–11 and their relation to actual events have been debated over many years, but here they will be considered only from the point of view of their literary form (Documents **3, 32, 33**).

With Genesis 11:27 the reader enters the world of the Patriarchs: Abraham, Isaac, Jacob and Joseph. Abraham sets out from Ur in Babylonia and travels to Syria–Palestine. There his successors and the tribe founded by him remain until Isaac's old age when, following Joseph, they travel to Egypt. The historical worth of these narratives and the dates involved are another area of debate. None of the Hebrews named in them is known from any other source, though the four kings against whom Abraham is described as fighting in Genesis 14 have plausible names for the second millennium BC. Despite a variety of views, the main consensus is to place the Patriarchs in the period from about 2000 to 1650 BC.

In terms of the chronological chart (p.17) this means that Abraham would have been in Babylonia in the Old Babylonian period and would have travelled to Syria (Harran) and then to Palestine in the Middle Bronze Age. The Israelites appear to have remained as semi-nomads, not settling in any cities, very much in the manner of the Hapiru group (see Documents **4, 7, 9**), to which they apparently belonged.

The move into Egypt fits plausibly into the Second Intermediate period in Egypt, the time when the Hyksos rulers had considerable influence in Palestine, and the Exodus and conquest of Palestine can be placed in the time of the Egyptian New Kingdom, specifically during the XIXth Dynasty (see Documents **10–12**), the end of the Late Bronze Age in Palestine.

Israelite history was thereafter largely enacted in Palestine. There the Israelites inevitably adopted many elements of the local culture and this included the language (see Document **4**) and alphabetic writing, which was already established in the area by the latter part of the second millennium BC (see Documents **5, 6, 14, 25**), and also items of material culture (cf. Document **24**), even those connected with the worship of the Temple (Document **13**). The period of the Divided Monarchy is illuminated by many inscriptions, and other antiquities from Assyria (Documents **15, 16, 19, 23, 26–31**), Babylonia (Documents **40, 42, 43**), and from other areas outside Israel and Judah (Documents **18, 34, 35**) as well as from Palestine itself (Documents **21, 22, 25, 36–39, 41**). Samaria lost its independence to the Assyrians in 722 BC, followed by deportations (the 'Lost Ten Tribes') (see Document **20**), and Judah fell to the Babylonians in 597 BC (see Document **43**) beginning the 'Exile' in Neo-Babylonian Babylonia (see Document **40**), but with the conquest of the Near East by the Achaemenain Persians, the Jews were able to return to Palestine (see Document **44**). The so-called Inter-Testamental Period falls within the Hellenistic period, a time when Seleucid and Ptolemaic rulers (descended from Seleucus and Ptolemy, two of the generals of Alexander the Great) (cf. Document **48**) were rivals for power in the area, and which saw the beginnings of Roman control.

As is well known the events of the New Testament took place against a background of Roman rule (see Documents **50–54**), and the spread of the church by such missionaries as Paul to Asia Minor, Greece and Rome all took place within the Roman Empire (Documents **56–58**). Greek was used throughout the eastern areas of the Empire, and continued as the official language of the Byzantine Empire, so it is not surprising that the New Testament documents have been handed down in Greek (see Documents **55, 59**).

The Ancient World *c.*3000 BC–*c.*250 AD

ITALY	GREECE	EGYPT	PALESTINE	MESOPOTAMIA	IRAN
Neolithic	Early Bronze Age	Predynastic	Early Bronze Age	Late Prehistoric	Early Bronze Age
		— 2600 —		— 2800 —	
		Old Kingdom		Early Dynastic (Sumerian)	
— 2200 —		— 2180 —	— 2200 —	— 2330 —	
		1 Intermediate		Akkadian Neo-Sumerian	
Copper Age	— 2000 —	— 2050 —	Middle Bronze Age	— 2000 —	— 2000 —
		Middle Kingdom →		Old Babylonian	Middle Bronze Age
	Middle Bronze Age	— 1780 —			
— 1700 —		2 Intermediate		— 1600 —	— 1600 —
Early Bronze Age	— 1550 —	— 1600 —	— 1550 —	Kassite	
— 1500 —		New Kingdom →	Late Bronze Age	— 1350 —	Late Bronze Age
Middle Bronze Age	Late Bronze Age (Mycenaean)			Middle Assyrian	
— 1200 —			— 1200 —		
Late Bronze Age	— 1100 —	— 1085 —	Iron Age I		
— 1000 —	Dark Age		— 1000 —	— 1000 —	
	— 900 —		Iron Age II (Monarchy)	Assyrian Empire	Iron Age
Early Iron Age	Geometric	Late Period	— 722 —		
	Orientalising			← 612	
Etruscans	Archaic		586 — ← Neo-Babylonian		— 549 —
— 509 —		— 525 —	— 539 —	— 539 —	
	— 480 —			← Achaemenian	
	Classical				
	— 332 —	— 332 —	— 332 —	— 330 —	— 327 —
Roman Republic	Hellenistic →				— 240 —
	— 146 —			— 141 —	
— 27 —	— 27 —	— 30 —	— 64 —		Parthian
			AD 44 —		
	Roman Empire				AD 224 —
				AD 240 —	Sassanian

Map of the Ancient World

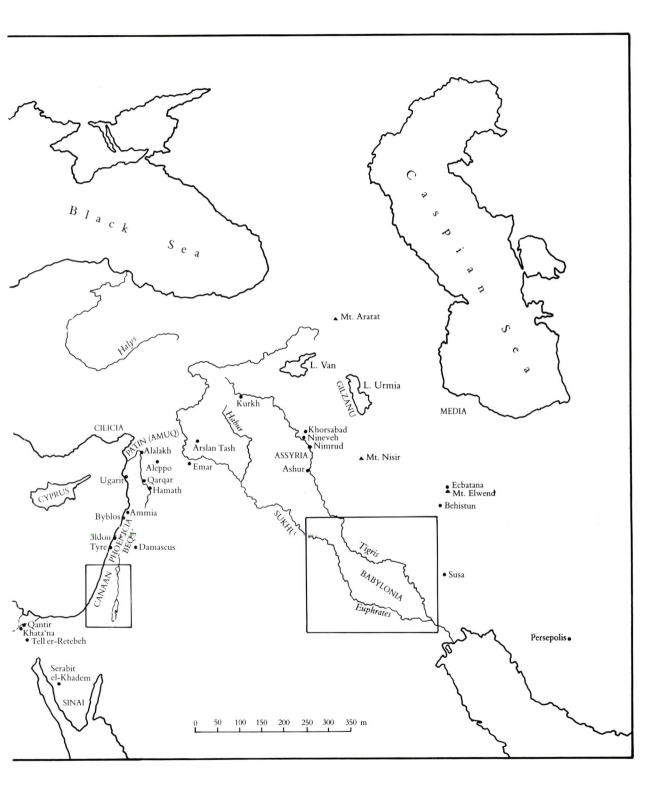

B l a c k   S e a

Halys

Mt. Ararat

L. Van

L. Urmia

GILZANU

MEDIA

C a s p i a n   S e a

Kurkh

CILICIA

PATIN (AMUQ)

Alalakh

Arslan Tash

Khorsabad
Nineveh
Nimrud

ASSYRIA

Aleppo

Emar

Ashur

Mt. Nisir

Ugarit

Qarqar

Hamath

Habur

Ecbatana
Mt. Elwend

Behistun

CYPRUS

Byblos

Ammia

SUKHU

Sidon

Tyre

PHOENICIA

BEQA'

Damascus

CANAAN

Tigris

Susa

BABYLONIA

Euphrates

Persepolis

Qantir
Khata'na
Tell er-Retebeh

Serabit
el-Khadem

SINAI

0   50   100   150   200   250   300   350 m

The Monarchy c.1000 BC–500 BC

EGYPT	JUDAH	ISRAEL	ARAM (Damascus)	ASSYRIA	BABYLONIA
	c.1000 David				
	c.967 Solomon	c.965			
945 Shoshenq	931 Rehoboam				
924	913 Abijah	Jeroboam I			
Osorkon I	911	910 Nadab			
		909 Baasha	c.900		
	Asa	886 Elah			
889		885 Zimri	Ben-Hadad I		
		885 Omri		884	
		874		Ashurnasirpal II	
	870 — 867	Ahab			
	Jehoshaphat	853 Ahaziah	c.860	859	
		852	Ben-Hadad II (Adad-idri)	Shalmaneser III	
	848 Jehoram	Joram	c.843		
841	841	841 Jehu		824	
	Jehoash	814 Jehoahaz	Hazael	Shamshi-Adad V	
		798	c.805	811 Adad-nirari III	
	796	Jehoash	Ben-Hadad III		
	Amaziah	782		783 Shalmaneser IV	
	767	Jeroboam II	c.773	7/3 Ashur-dan III	
		753 Zechariah		755	
	Uzziah	752 Shallum	Hadianu	Ashur-nirari	
		752 Menahem	c.750	745	
		742 Pekahiah			

EGYPT	JUDAH	ISRAEL	ARAM (Damascus)	ASSYRIA	BABYLONIA
	— 740 —	— 740 —	Rezin	Tiglath-pileser III	
	Jotham	Pekah			
	— 732 —	— 732 —	— 732 —		
		Hoshea		— 727 —	— 729 —
	Ahaz			Shalmaneser V	— 727 —
		— 722 —		— 722 —	— 722 —
— 716 —	— 716 —			Sargon	Merodach-baladan II
					— 710 —
				— 705 —	— 705 —
Shabako					— 703 —
					Marduk-zakir-shumi
	Hezekiah				— 703 —
				Sennacherib	Merodach-baladan II
					— 703 —
— 702 —					
Shebitku					
— 690 —					
	— 687 —			— 681 —	— 681 —
Taharqa				Esarhaddon	
				— 669 —	— 669 —
	Manasseh				— 668 —
— 664 —					Shamash-shum-ukin
				Ashurbanipal	— 648 —
	— 643 —				Kandalanu
	Amon				
	— 641 —			— 627 —	— 625 —
	Josiah			— 612 —	
— 610 —	— 609 —				
	Jehoahaz				Nabopolassar
	— 609 —				
Necho II	Jehoiaqim				— 605 —
	— 598 —				
	Jehoiakin				
	— 597 —				
— 595 —	Zedekiah				Nebuchadnezzar
	— 587 —				
	Gedaliah				
	— 586 —				

Palestine in New Testament Times

	ROME	JUDAEA, SAMARIA and IDUMAEA	ITURAEA and TRACHONITIS	GALILEE and PERAEA

ROMAN PROTECTORATE

— 37 —

40
30 — 29 —
Herod the Great (King)
20
10
BC — 4 — 4 — 4 —
0
AD
Archelaus (Ethnarch)   Philip (Tetrarch)   Herod Antipas (Tetrarch)

Augustus

— 6 —
ROMAN RULE
10
— 14 —
20
Tiberius
— 26 —
30
Pilate
— 34 —
— 37 —   — 36 —   — 37 —
Caligula
40 — 41 —   — 41 —   Herod Agrippa I (King)   — 39 —
— 44 —   — 44 —   — 44 —
Claudius
ROMAN RULE
50
— 54 —   — 53 —
  — 56 —
60
Nero   Herod Agrippa II (King)
— 66 —   — 66 —   — 66 —
— 68 —

22

The Documents

The following pages contain numbered 'Documents'. These refer to antiquities, whether inscribed or not, which have a bearing on Biblical Archaeology. They have been arranged chronologically so as to give an impression of their relative dates, and also to show how literary motifs such as a flood story are found in texts over a very long period (Document **3** and **33**). Within this they can be classified in various ways, the most obvious divisions being between: (a) those inscriptions which give information specifically relevant to Israelite history (Documents **12, 15, 16, 18, 26, 27, 43**); (b) those objects and inscriptions which illustrate or bear on the cultural milieu, or background of the contemporary world (Documents **4, 7, 9, 11, 13, 14, 21, 22, 24, 28, 34–39, 41, 44, 48, 49, 54, 56–58**); (c) those inscriptions which represent literary forms or types parallel to passages in the Biblical text (Documents **3, 28, 32, 33, 48, 55**); and (d) those inscriptions which illustrate the transmission of the actual Biblical text (Documents **55, 59, 60**).

The collections of the British Museum and British Library are rich in material which helps to illuminate the Bible, but three antiquities from other collections are included (Documents **12, 18, 48**) because of their particular relevance, and another two because they have been misunderstood in the past (**1** and **17**) and it will be useful once and for all to set the record straight.

The objects have been selected in order to give an idea of the kind of illumination which antiquities can give to the text of the Bible. This is not always very startling but an attempt has been made to draw out the direct contributions that they can make, and when appropriate the occasion has been taken to pursue secondary matters raised by them. The result is not systematic, but this may serve to show some of the limitations of the study of Biblical Archaeology.

'Temptation Seal'

This cylinder seal was related to the temptation of Eve in the Garden of Eden (Gen. 3:1–13) by George Smith of the British Museum (1840–76). Of it, he wrote:

One striking and important specimen of early type in the British Museum has two figures sitting one on each side of a tree, holding out their hands to the fruit, while at the back of one is stretched a serpent. We know well that in these early sculptures none of these figures were chance devices, but all represented events or supposed events, and figures in their legends; thus it is evident that a form of the story of the Fall, similar to that of Genesis, was known in early times in Babylonia.

Such an interpretation has been given many times since. In fact the seal belongs to a well-known genre of the Akkadian and post-Akkadian periods in Mesopotamia (twenty-third and twenty-second centuries BC), and shows a seated male figure, identified by his headdress as a deity, facing a female worshipper. Both figures are fully clothed. The date-palm between them and the snake may have had fertility significance and there is no reason to connect the scene with the Adam and Eve story.

'Temptation Seal' from Mesopotamia; 23rd century BC. Greenstone facies; ht 2.71cm. WA 89326

Ziggurat at Ur

Most of the important cities of ancient Mesopotamia had temple towers, that is, stepped pyramids, surmounted by small temples, as part of their main religious areas. The Babylonian and Assyrian word for one of these towers was *ziqqurratu* 'temple tower', and this has been adopted in English as ziggurat.

One of the best preserved examples is that excavated by Sir Leonard Woolley (1880–1960) on behalf of the British Museum and the University Museum, Philadelphia, at Ur in southern Iraq. The surviving part here illustrated has roughly the form which it had in the time of Ur-Nammu, king of Ur 2112–2095 BC, but remains of later date show that in the time of the last Babylonian king, Nabonidus, 555–539 BC, it was rebuilt to a considerably greater height (see Document 42). Moreover there can be little doubt that Ur-Nammu's structure contains previous towers of decreasing size going back to a small temple, probably on a platform, of much earlier date, now buried in the core. This is clear from excavations at other sites such as Eridu, but it cannot be verified at Ur without destroying the ziggurat as it now survives.

The Mesopotamian ziggurat as a type has long been connected with the Tower of Babel described in Genesis 11:1–9. There it is located in the land of Shinar, Hebrew *šin'ār*, which is shown by its use in other contexts to have referred to 'Babylonia' (cf. Isaiah 11:11; and Zech 5:11 both rendered in the Septuagint by *Babulōnos*), and not 'Sumer', Akkadian *šumeru*, which was only the southern part of Babylonia. Babylonia embraced the area which before 2000 BC had consisted of Sumer in the south and Akkad in the north, the city of Babylon actually lying in Akkad rather than Sumer.

The 'tower' in Genesis is a *migdāl*, literally 'big place', and it is said to have been called *bābel*, the name applied elsewhere in the Old Testament to the city of Babylon. There seems no reason, therefore, not to connect the *migdāl* of *bābel* with the ziggurat at Babylon, represented today largely by a water-and-reed-filled hole in the ground, the baked bricks of which it was built having been taken for use elsewhere.

The Old Testament explains that the tower was named *bābel* because it was there that Yahweh (see Document 41) 'confused' (*bālal*) the languages of the earth (Gen. 11:9), while the Akkadian name of the city *bab-ili* means 'gate of the god'. The apparently incorrect explanation given by Genesis may have been a gloss added by a later scribe.

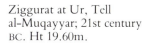

Ziggurat at Ur, Tell al-Muqayyar; 21st century BC. Ht 19.60m.

Atrahasis Epic

Genesis was known to the Hebrews as *bĕrē 'šit* (in (the) 'beginning') from its first word, and in the same way the Babylonians referred to one of their compositions as *inuma ilu awilum*, 'when the gods like men', from its opening words. Copies of this composition, known today as The Atrahasis Epic (after its hero of the same name), have survived from the Old, Middle and Neo-Babylonian and the Neo-Assyrian periods, showing that it was copied and re-copied over the centuries. The most complete version, in which over 1200 lines of text divided into three tablets are preserved, dates from about the seventeenth century BC. It is likely that it was originally composed sometime in the nineteenth or eighteenth century BC, by an author who made use of existing traditions. It begins by outlining the structure of the universe in which the heavens are ruled by the god Anu, the earth by Enlil, and the subterranean sweet water ocean by Enki. Enlil puts the minor gods to work on earth, digging canals, farming the land and carrying out other tasks but after forty years they rebel and refuse to work. In response Enki, who appears as a wise conciliator, suggests that man be created to take over the work and this proposal is accepted by the gods. Man is made by the goddess Mami, with the help of Enki, by modelling him from clay mixed with spittle, and with the blood of a god We or Weila, otherwise unknown, who is killed for the purpose. The human race is put to work and it multiplies, until the noise disturbs Enlil's sleep. He therefore decides to destroy man, and sends first a plague, then a famine, and then a drought, and finally a flood, but each time Enki instructs Atrahasis, who now appears in the story, on how to mitigate the effects of these disasters. He gives him seven days warning of the flood, and tells him to build a boat. Atrahasis builds the boat, loads it with his possessions and animals and birds, and after a banquet embarks and is preserved while all the rest of mankind is destroyed. When the gods see the result of the flood they realise that there are no men to produce food for offerings to them, and come to regret it. Here there is a gap in the manuscript so no details of the landing of the boat survive, but the epic ends with Atrahasis making an offering to the gods, and Enlil finally accepting the existence of man.

The points of particular interest in this composition from the Biblical point of view are the Creation of man and the Flood. The combination of clay with blood in the account of the creation of man reflects similar ideas to those found in the Old Testament where man is described as having been formed of 'dust' or 'earth' to which he would return (Gen. 3:19), and where it is stated that 'the life is in the blood' (Lev.17:11). In other respects the Creation accounts in Genesis and Atrahasis have little in common.

There are clearly similarities between the account of the Flood in Atrahasis, as well as others known in Mesopotamian literature, notably a Sumerian version of about the seventeenth to sixteenth century BC from Nippur, and that preserved in the Gilgamesh Epic (Document 33), and Noah's Flood in Genesis (Gen. 6–8). The names of the heroes of course differ, Atrahasis, Ziusudra (Sumerian version), Utnapishtim (Gilgamesh-Epic) and Noah, but the general outlines are comparable, and the relationships have been much discussed. In general three hypotheses are possible. (a) The Hebrew account was borrowed from Mesopotamia. In the days when the main cuneiform version known was that of the seventh century BC in the Gilgamesh Epic (Document **33**) the theory held that the Hebrews adopted it during the Exile. With the discovery of the previous versions, it became possible to assume a borrowing in the second millennium, perhaps in the time of the Patriarchs. (b) The Mesopotamian accounts were borrowed from the Hebrews. (c) Both accounts derive from a common original. In connection with this it is worth noting that it has been argued that the corpus of Sumerian literature as it existed in the Early Dynastic period of the mid-third millennium BC, (largely

preserved today in sources of the early second millennium), did not include a flood account. The great Sumerian King-List which mentions a Flood in some versions does not do so in all manuscripts, and the evidence is lacking to settle whether it was an original element. Equally, data is not available to decide whether or not a common earlier account might have existed, since this could well carry the question back to a time before the invention of writing.

On present evidence the second of the three hypothesese, that the Babylonians borrowed their flood accounts from the Hebrews, is extremely unlikely and, in the final analysis, the decision between the other two is a question of individual choice on the basis of personal presuppositions.

Atrahasis Epic, probably from Sippar (Abu Habba); *c.* 17th century BC. Ht 22.6cm. WA 78942+

Statue of Idri-mi

This very stylised statue was found together with its base at Tell Atshanah, ancient Alalakh, by Sir Leonard Woolley in 1939. It depicts Idri-mi, the ruler of Alalakh in north Syria, c. 1550 BC, and has particular interest because it bears, virtually all over it, a cuneiform inscription in 104 lines giving his autobiography. He states that he was born in Aleppo, when trouble arose at home he escaped first to Emar then to Ammia in 'Canaan', and finally he took refuge with the 'Hapiru warriors'. After seven years he was able to return and repossess Alalakh, which had formed part of the kingdom of Aleppo in his father's time, and the inscription goes on to give an account of a treaty concluded with Barattarna, king of Mitanni; tribute received from vassals; a campaign against the Hittites to the north, and his establishment of firm rule in his kingdom.

Idri-mi's movements from city to city, and his seven years' sojourn, apparently away from any city, is reminiscent of the wanderings of some of the Hebrew Patriarchs, but this inscription is also interesting in containing the earliest known reference to Canaan, here written *ma-at ki-in-a-nim*[ki], 'land of Canaan' (lines 18 and 19 on the right arm of the statue), though 'Canaanites' are mentioned as early as the eighteenth century BC, in a letter from Mari. Canaan is, of course, known from the Old Testament where it is written *kĕna'an*, sometimes in the phrase *'eres-kĕna'an*, 'land of Canaan', (e.g. Gen. 35:6; 42:5; 44:8 etc.) where *'eres* corresponds to Akkadian *mātu*, 'land'. Outside the Bible the usage of the name in Egyptian texts (kn'n), the Amarna Letters (*kinaḫḫi*) and alphabetic cuneiform tablets from Ras Shamra, ancient Ugarit, suggest that in the second half of the second millennium BC the name Canaan described the area adjacent to the Mediterranean coast from about Gaza in the south to Al-Arida (more or less level with Homs) in the north and extending inland to the Jordan and Beqa' valleys, that is roughly the area occupied by modern Israel and Lebanon. Idri-mi's travels took him to the northern end of this territory. This roughly corresponds to the area described in Numbers 34:3–6 and Joshua 15:1–4, with the difference that these accounts include a considerable extension to the east in the northern half, including the area centring on Damascus. It may be appropriate to say therefore that the territory defined in Numbers and Joshua is 'Canaan plus'.

The inscription is also interesting in describing Idri-mi's hosts during seven years of his exile as 'Hapiru warriors', written *ṣābē*[pl] [amīlu]SA.GAZ (line 27, on his knees, to the right of the 'lion's tail' of his garment). In this, *ṣābē*, plural of *ṣābu*, 'troop', is cognate with Hebrew *ṣābā'*, 'army' familiar in the plural *seba'ot* from the liturgical title 'Lord (God) of Sabaoth (Hosts)'. *Amīlu* is the determinative preceding the name of a people, in this case SA.GAZ. The pronounciation of this name, conventionally transcribed in capital letters because the two signs with which it was written were ideographic rather than phonetic, was quite different. What this pronounciation was is indicated by other evidence. Among the texts from Ugarit a list of places written in Akkadian (syllabic) cuneiform includes the name [ālu]*ḫal-bi* [amīlu]SAG.GAZ, 'Halbi of the SA.GAZ people' and there is good reason for identifying this with a place-name written in Ugaritic (alphabetic) cuneiform as *ḫlb 'prm*. This suggests the equation SA.GAZ = *'pr*, and this conclusion is borne out by the Amarna letters where the letters from Jerusalem refer to a group of troublesome people as *ḫa-pi-ru*, while several letters from other places refer to SA.GAZ in similar contexts and roles (see below Document 7). On the basis of this and other similar evidence it is generally accepted that the name SA.GAZ was pronounced *ḫa-pi-ru* or something similar. These people are referred to in a considerable number of texts ranging in date from the late third millennium until the fourteenth century BC, from Mesopotamia, Asia Minor, Syria and Egypt (as *'pr*),

Statue of Idri-mi from Tell
Atshanah, ancient Alalakh;
16th century BC. Magnesite
(plinth, dolomite); ht of
statue 104cm. WA 130738

the people being described as labourers, mercenaries, brigands or the like, their particular role varying from place to place. By and large the name Hapiru seems to have been a descriptive rather than an ethnic term, rather like 'road people' in more recent times.

A question much debated is whether the name *hapiru/'pr* has any connection with Old Testament *'ibrî*, 'Hebrew'. Though the phonemic correspondence is not close enough to make this certain, it cannot be ruled out. In the Old Testament the *'ibrî* appear in various categories. In Exodus 21:2–6 they are slaves of Israelites, in 1 Samuel 14:21 mercenary soldiers serving the Philistines, and a common usage is one in which non-Israelites use it to refer to Israelites (eg. Gen. 39:14, 17; 41:12; Ex. 1:16; 2:6; 1 Sam. 4:6, 9; 13:19; 14:11; 29:3), and Israelites use it referring to themselves when speaking to non-Israelites (eg. Gen. 40:15; Ex. 1:19; 2:7; 3:18; 5:3; 7:16; 9:1, 13). These passages all refer to the time before the Israelites were fully settled in Palestine, and a possible interpretation of the evidence is that the Biblical 'Hebrews' were simply one small sub-group of the larger Hapiru class, and that it would be true to say that while all Hebrews of that period could be seen as part of the Hapiru, not all Hapiru were Hebrews (see also Document 9). In the past the references to Hapiru in the Amarna letters (see Document 7), have been taken to indicate that the Biblical Hebrews were in Palestine by the fourteenth century BC, but the possibility that the Hebrews were just one sub-group of a much larger class suggests that there is no reason to identify them directly with the Hapiru of the Amarna Letters.

The political situation in the Near East changed by the first millennium BC, and the Hapiru are no longer heard of, but the name 'Hebrew' continued to be used by the Hebrews (eg. Jer. 34:9; 2 Cor. 11:22), and while what we now call the Hebrew language was earlier referred to as the 'lip of Canaan' (*śĕpat kĕna'an*; Is. 19:18) and was subsequently known as *yĕhûdît*, 'Jewish' (2 Ki. 18:26; Neh. 13:24); it came in Biblical times to be called *lāšôn 'ibrît*, 'Hebrew tongue'. In the New Testament the Greek word *hebraisti* refers to the Hebrew language in Revelation 9:11 and 16:16, but elsewhere this same term (Jn. 5:2; 19:13, 17, 20), as well as *hebraios* (Acts 21:40; 22:2; 26:14) and *hebraikos* (Lk. 23:38), all rendered 'Hebrew' in the Authorised and Revised Versions, probably refer to Aramaic, the common language of Palestine in New Testament times.

Inscribed Sphinx

Inscribed sphinx from
Serabit al-Khadem, Sinai;
15th century BC.
Sandstone; lth 24.7cm.
WA 41748

Stone sphinx, discovered by Flinders Petrie (1853–1942) in the Hathor Temple at Sarabit al-Khaden, an Egyptian turquoise mining centre in the Sinai Peninsula. This and a number of other statues as well as rock faces found at or near the same site bear inscriptions in a sub-hieroglyphic linear script which has been plausibly deciphered as an early form of the alphabet, referred to for convenience as Proto-Sinaitic and dated to the fifteenth century BC.

The part of the inscription on the side of the sphinx shown in the photograph is not entirely clear, but the last five characters, reading from the left, are possibly derived from the Egyptian hieroglyphs for oxgoad-house-eye-oxgoad-owner's mark. When the probable later Semitic alphabetic values derived from the initial consonants of the names of these objects are substituted, l-b꞉-l-t, the reading *lb'lt* 'to Ba'lat', emerges, in which Ba'lat, 'Lady' is a plausible epithet for the goddess Hathor, and *l-*, is the preposition 'to', familiar in Hebrew. When this same principle is applied throughout the inscriptions, the language which is found, very sparsely attested, it is true, has sufficient features to place it in the West Semitic group, though whether Northwest of Southwest Semitic is disputed.

The main interest of this Sphinx and the other Proto-Sinaitic inscriptions is, however, the evidence it gives of an early form of the alphabet.

There are fragmentary suggestions that an early form of the alphabet was in use before this, but the Proto-Sinaitic inscriptions provide the earliest substantial body of material. The location in Sinai and the similarity in form to Egyptian hieroglyphics suggest that the developer(s) of this script borrowed both the idea of writing and the forms of the letters from the Eyptian but assigned his/their own values to them.

An alphabet, albeit a cuneiform one, was extensively used at Ugarit in the fourteenth century BC. This implies the existence of a linear (as distinct from a cuneiform) script well in use by this time, because the Ugaritic characters are clearly specially devised to suit the cuneiform mode of writing, on the basis of a different existing script.

Writing is mentioned frequently in the Bible, from the time of Moses on. Since he is said to have grown up in the Egyptian royal court he would be presumed to have known the Egyptian language and script, and this may be what the references to writing in the Pentateuch (Ex. 17:14; 24:4; 34:27, 28; Num. 33:2; Deut. 31:9, 22, 24) signify, though the use of an alphabet cannot be ruled out. In view of the clear evidence of the knowledge of cuneiform script in Egypt in the fourteenth century (Documents 7 and 8), it is also possible that this would have been known to a well educated member of the Egyptian royal court.

The Alphabet

A pictographic alphabet was already in existence by the middle of the second millennium BC (Document 5), and in the following centuries the pictographs were simplified to what may be called a linear alphabet. The accompanying chart shows a selection of forms of the alphabetic script, beginning with the Proto-Sinaitic series (column 2), and giving a selection of west Semitic versions from the eleventh to fifth centuries BC, (columns 3–10), then the Qumran and medieval Hebrew scripts (columns 11–12), and the standard Greek alphabet (column 13).

The early alphabetic script was adopted for use in writing a number of west Semitic languages, principally Phoenician, Hebrew and Aramaic. The examples included in the chart do not show a smooth line of development because the different branches diverged palaeographically over the centuries. A complete chart would show an example of each branch for each century, but such detail is inappropriate here. The spread of representation is as follows (the numbers representing columns on the chart):

Century	Phoenician	Hebrew	Aramaic
11th	3		
10th	4		
9th		5	
8th		6	
7th		7	
6th		8	
5th			9, 10

The Phoenician branch is the earliest represented, being found in brief inscriptions in the thirteenth century, and particularly on inscribed arrowheads in the twelfth and eleventh centuries (column 3 = Document 14), but from the tenth century the Hebrew and from the ninth century the Aramaic scripts developed along their own divergent lines. This is clear between columns 8 and 9, the former being Hebrew, the latter representing the point reached along a different line of development by the Aramaic script in the fifth century BC.

The examples of script have been taken, when possible, from Documents contained in this book, but Column 4 uses the inscription on the sarcophagus of Ahiram, ruler of the Byblos, as representing a clear form of the tenth century Phoenician script.

Column 9 represents the fifth century Aramaic lapidary script (Document 46) not every character being used, and Column 10 is included to show the form used in ink on papyrus. This illustrates the fact that the later Hebrew 'square' script, as represented in a ninth century AD manuscript (column 12 = Document 60), follows the Aramaic tradition of about the time of the Exile. This is natural since Aramaic had become the *lingua franca* of the time, and the Jews in Exile in Babylon would have had to use it. The Old Hebrew script (columns 5–8) was only used very selectively after the Return (see Document 60). The similarity between the traditional Hebrew letter forms and those of the fifth century Aramaic script is clear in the case of *b, h, ḥ, ṭ, q, r, š* and *t*.

It may be noted that both in the Old Hebrew script of the Sixth century BC (column 8), and to a lesser extent in the later square script (column 10), the *d* and *r* are similar. A clear instance of a confusion arising from this similarity is found in Genesis 10:4 where among the descendants of *yāwān,* 'Javan' (Ionians), *dōdānîm,* 'Dodanim', is listed. The Greek Old Testament (Septuagint) gives the name *rhodioi* at this point and this is supported by the parallel passage in 1 Chronicles 1:7 which

reads *rôdānîm*, 'Rodanim' (Rhodians), giving a meaning which is appropriate in association with Ionians, and other Aegean peoples. It is thus clear that the graphic similarity between *d* and *r* had led to a scribal error in the course of copying.

The Greek script is included in column 13 since it is used in some of the later Documents(48, 54–59). Different languages have different sets of significant sounds (phonemes), English, for instance relying on the difference between *l* and *r* to distinguish meanings, as in 'lot' and 'rot', which Japanese, as is well known, does not make this distinction. In the same way in the Semitic languages significant differences in meaning are marked as between the gutteral consonants *' h ḥ* and *c*, between the basic and emphatic consonant pairs *t-ṭ, s-ṣ* and *k-q*, and among the sibilants *s, ṣ* and *š*. At the same time, while vowels were, of course, pronounced, they were of less significance in distinguishing meaning, and indeed they were not represented in the west Semitic scripts until the Christian era. The Greeks, on the other hand, needed to record vowels in their inscriptions, and had no need of so many gutterals, emphatics or sibilants. Thus, when they encountered the Phoencian alphabet in the course of trade, they adopted it, keeping the sounds that were useful to them, but assigning new sound values to the symbols which the Phoenicians used for sounds that they did not need. In the Ionian area, the alphabet of which came eventually to override the different alphabets of others areas, the Phoenician symbol for *'*, became *a, h,* became *e, ḥ* became *ē, ḥt* became *th, y* became *i, s* became *x(ks), '* became *o, š* became *s,* and five further symbols were added at the end. Some areas took over the Semitic *w* in a form like F (the digamma; cf. the form of *w* in column 6), but this was not used in the Ionian script. It may be noted, somewhat tangentially, since Hebrew *yāwān* has been mentioned above, that a passage mentioning this name in Homer in the form *iaones* (Iliad 13:685) is one of a class which presented scholars with difficulties of poetic metre, until a suggestion was made in the eighteenth century that in the spoken language words such as this included another consonant not represented in the written text. The subsequent discovery of the digamma in inscriptions has supported this suggestion and made it probable that *iaones* would have been pronounced *iawones*, and would indeed have been so written if the alphabets in the Ionian tradition had retained the digamma.

The columns in the chart represent:

1 Phonetic Value
2 Proto-Sinaitic Script (Document 5), 15th century BC.
3 Arrow-head (Document 14), 11th century BC, Phoenician.
4 Sarcophagus of Ahiram ruler of Byblos, 10th century BC, Phoenician.
5 Moabite Stone (Document 18), 9th century BC. Moabite, though strictly speaking this was so close to Hebrew as to be virtually indistinguishable.
6 Royal Stamped Jar Handles (Document 22), 8th century BC, Hebrew.
7 Royal Steward Inscription (Document 25), 7th century BC, Hebrew.
8 Lachish Ostracon (Document 41), 6th century BC, Hebrew.
9 Parshandata Seal (Document 46), 5th century BC, Aramaic.
10 Aramaic Papyri from Hermopolis, Egypt, 5th century BC, Aramaic.
11 Qumran Manuscript, 1st century BC, Hebrew.
12 Hebrew Pentateuch (Document 60) 9th century AD.
13 Greek Alphabet.

1	2	3	4	5	6	7	8	9	10	11	12	13
ʾ / a	𐤀	𐤀	𐤀	𐤀		𐤀	𐤀	𐤀	𐤀	𐤀	𐤀	A
b	☐	◁	𐤁	𐤁	𐤁	𐤁	𐤁	𐤁	𐤁	𐤁	𐤁	B
g	∟		𐤂	𐤂					∧	𐤂	𐤂	Γ
d	𐤃	△	△	△		◁	◀	𐤃	𐤃	𐤃	𐤃	Δ
h	𐤄	𐤄	∃	∃	𐤄	𐤄	𐤄		𐤄	𐤄	𐤄	E
w	𐤅		Y	Y	𐤅	𐤅	𐤅		𐤅	𐤅	𐤅	(F)
z			I	I	𐤆	𐤆	𐤆		𐤆	𐤆	𐤆	Z
ḥ / ē	⊞	⊟	𐤇	𐤇	𐤇	𐤇		𐤇	𐤇	𐤇	𐤇	H
ṭ / th			⊕	⊘					𐤈	𐤈	𐤈	Θ
y / i	𐤉		𐤉	𐤉		𐤉	𐤉		𐤉	𐤉	𐤉	I
k	ᴟ		𐤊	𐤊	𐤊	𐤊	𐤊		𐤊	𐤊	𐤊	K
l	𐤋	𐤋	𐤋	𐤋	𐤋	𐤋	𐤋		𐤋	𐤋	𐤋	Λ
m	〰		𐤌	𐤌	𐤌	𐤌	𐤌	𐤌	𐤌	𐤌	𐤌	M

1	2	3	4	5	6	7	8	9	10	11	12	13
n												N
s												
x													Ξ
ʿ													
o													O
p													Π
ṣ													
q													Q
r													P
š													
ś													
s													Σ
t													T
u													Y
ph													Φ
kh													X
ps													Ψ
ō													Ω

Letter from Yapaḫu

The Amarna Letters, of which this is one, are clay tablets inscribed in cuneiform, mostly in the Babylonian language, with messages to the Egyptian Pharaohs Amenhotep III and Amenhotep IV. They were discovered in 1887 at el-Amarna in Egypt (the site of Akhet-Aten), which was the new capital to which Amenhotep IV moved to establish a religious reform. This was in worship of Aten, the god of the sun-disk, as the sole supreme being and in honour of whom Amenhotep changed his name to Akhen-Aten.

Over 350 tablets were found, of which the largest collections are in the Cairo Museum, the British Museum and the Berlin Museum. They are mainly letters from the contemporary Hittite, Mitannian and Babylonian kings, and from subject rulers in Palestine, Phoenicia and Syria. They date from the fourteenth century BC, a time, not long before the Exodus, when Egyptian power in Palestine was waning, and they contain pleas from the subject rulers for help against lawless bands, and also against rulers of neighbouring cities who they frequently accuse of disloyalty to Egypt. The present letter is from Yapahu the ruler of Gezer who acknowledges a message from the Pharaoh and asks for help against a marauding group of Hapiru (see Document 4). The text, typical of these letters, runs:

To the king, my lord, my god, my sun, the sun in the sky. Thus [says] Yapaḫu, governor of Gezer, your servant, the dust at your feet, the groom of your horses. I surely fall at the feet of the king, my lord, my god, my sun, the sun in the sky, seven times and seven times, on the stomach and on the back. I have surely heard the words of the messenger of the king my lord. May the king, my lord, the sun in the sky, care for his land. Since the Ḥapiru (SA.GAZ) are stronger than us, may the king, my lord, help me to escape from the Ḥapiru, so that the Ḥapiru do not destroy us.

Below Letter from Yapahu ruler of Gezer from el-Amarna, Egypt; 14th century BC. Baked clay; ht 10.8cm. WA E 29832

Letter from Biridiya

Part of a letter from Biridiya the rule of Megiddo, to the Egyptian Pharaoh, explaining to him his failure to convey a prisoner to Egypt, and accusing a man named Zurata of having received ransom money for the prisoner.

This letter contains a feature familiar from several of the Amarna letters, in which the scribe supplies translations of some of the Akkadian words. The majority of the letters are in Akkadian in a vulgar form of the Middle Babylonian dialect, and the translations or glosses are placed next to the Akkadian words, separated from them by oblique wedges. The present letter has two such glosses, the second one giving a good illustration of the kind of thing involved. In line 35 where the ransom money is referred to, Biridiya says that Zurata received the money 'in his hand'. In the main Akkadian text this is written:

i			
na	} i-na	in	
qāti			
ti	} qāti(ti)-šu	his hand	
šu			

Though *qātu*, 'hand', is written with a word sign, in which its pictographic origin can still be recognised, the 'phonetic complement' *ti* shows that it is to be read *qāti* with the *-i* ending following the preposition *ina*. To this the scribe supplies the gloss *ba-di-ú*, of which the affiliations may be seen by comparison with Hebrew *bĕyādô* 'in his hand', (eg. Gen. 22:6), *bĕ* (in) + *yād* (hand) + *ô* (his). This does not mean that the language of the glosses is early Hebrew, only that it belongs to the same general linguistic group which, after 1000 BC, is recognisable in Phoenician, Hebrew, Moabite and Edomite, and is labelled for convenience the Canaanite branch of the north west Semitic group of languages. The evidence of these glosses together with that from the Ugaritic texts, also of the fourteenth and thirteenth centuries (though the classification of Ugaritic is much debated and Ugarit itself lay outside ancient Canaan) gives point to the description of Hebrew as 'the language of Canaan' (Is. 19:18; see also under Document 4 above). It seems that the Hebrews adopted the language of Canaan either during the the Patriarchal wanderings in Palestine-Syria or at the time of the Exodus and Conquest and that it developed into a distinct dialect over the centuries.

Left Letter from Biridiya ruler of Megiddo from el-Amarna, Egypt; 14th century BC. Baked clay; ht 9.8cm. WA E 29855

The Capture of Joppa

Among the compositions inscribed in Egyptian hieroglyphics on this papyrus is a story, or romance, puporting to describe an event in the Palestinian campaign of Tuthmosis III (1479–1425 BC). The beginning is damaged but the story describes how Tuthmosis's general Djehuty, having failed to capture the Palestinian city of Joppa by conventional means, succeeds in taking it by a ruse involving the introduction of two hundred men concealed in baskets.

This document, which is in any case fiction, has no direct bearing on the Old Testament, but it is reasonable to take it as reflecting the situation in Canaan in the last centuries before the Israelite conquest. Joppa, which was in the territory later assigned to the tribe of Dan (Josh. 19:46), is the only natural harbour on the coast between the Egyptian frontier and the bay of Acre. It is described as the port to which cedar wood from Lebanon for use in the building of Solomon's Temple was floated and from which it was transported overland to Jerusalem (2 Chron. 2:16) and as the port from which Jonah embarked for the west Mediterranean (Jon. 1:3).

A relevant element near the beginning of the surviving part of the story appears when the invading general asks the defenders to let his horses be brought into the town because outside they are vulnerable to the 'Apiru (*'pr*; the Egyptian writing of Hapiru). This is another appearance of these people, known from many other texts (see Document 4), and just as, for instance, references to gypsies in a Jane Austen novel give a valid impression of their place in eighteenth century England, so the reference to 'Apiru in this fictional work gives an idea of their role c. 1250 BC, if not in the fifteenth century.

The Capture of Joppa, said to be from Thebes, Egypt; *c.* 1300 BC. Papyrus; ht 20.3cm. E 10060 (Papyrus Harris 500)

Statue of Ramesses II

Ramesses II is portrayed here as a young man. He is identified by cartouches with his name on each shoulder and is shown wearing the combined crown of Upper and Lower Egypt and holding the crook and flail of kingship.

Ramesses II, who reigned for over half a century, was one of the great kings of the Nineteenth Dynasty. He conducted many military campaigns in Western Asia, and carried out numerous building operations throughout Egypt. Among these he was active in completing a royal residence begun in the east Delta by his father Sethos I, which he named Per-Ramesses 'House of Ramesses' in his own honour. This building work appears to correspond to that involving the Israelites during the 'oppression' (Ex 1:8–11). Coupled with the evidence of the Merneptah Stela (which implies that the Israelites were a wandering group in Palestine c.1208 BC, with a possible Exodus in the thirteenth century BC) this suggests Ramesses II as a possible Pharaoh of the Exodus. This matter is still debated however, and the evidence of destruction levels at Palestinian sites, which may be connected with the period of the Israelite conquest, does not lend itself to a simple conclusion.

Statue of Ramesses II, (1279–1212 BC) from Elephantine. Granite; ht 152cm. E 67

Brick of Ramesses II

This brick is made of Nile mud with chopped straw as a binder, and has been stamped with a seal bearing a cartouche containing hieroglyphics reading Usima'rē' setpenrē' part of the official name of Ramesses II. While the pharaoh of the Exodus is not named, being referred to in the Old Testament only as *par'ōh* (e.g. Ex. 1:11). Ramesses II is a strong contender (see Documents 10 and 12). Hebrew *par'ōh*, 'Pharaoh' is derived from Egyptian *pr-''*, 'Great House' which was used from at least the 14th century BC to refer to the king.

The Israelites are described as building 'store cities' at Pithom and Raamses with clay and brick (Ex. 1:11–14). That straw was regarded as a normal ingredient is shown by the imposition later on of the extra duty on the Israelites to collect their own straw for brick making (Ex. 5:6–13).

The cities referred to, Pithom, Hebrew *pitōm*, from Egyptian *pr-'itm* 'House of Atum' (or Aton-) and Raamses, Hebrew *ra'amsēs*, from Egyptian *(pr-)r'mss*, 'House of Ramesses', are possibly to be identified respectively with Tell er-Retabeh in the Wadi Tumilat and with an area on the Pelusiac branch of the Nile including Khata'na (with Tell ed-Dab'a) and Qantir.

Brick of Ramesses II (1279–1212 BC) from Thebes, presented by Lord Prudhoe in 1835. Mud and straw; lth 38cm. E 6020

Merneptah Stela

The granite stela of Amenophis III, re-used on the back, by Merneptah (1211–1202 BC), the successor of Ramesses II in the Egyptian Nineteenth Dynasty. The king is twice depicted at the top of the stela facing two representations of the god Amun-Re, and flanked by the gods Mut and Khonsu. Below is a twenty-eight line hieroglyphic text giving a series of hymns of victory, chiefly over the Lybians, in his fifth year, but including, near the end, celebration of triumph over various peoples of Western Asia, including Hatti (northern Syria), Canaan (southern Syria and Palestine; see Document 4), Ashkelon, Gezer, Yanoam (a city in northern Palestine), Israel, and Hurru (probably Palestine as a whole), in that order. All of these place names are written with the determinative for 'land' with the exception of Israel which has the determinative for 'people', so, assuming this writing to be intended and not a scribal mistake, it suggests that the Israelites were a wandering, unsettled, group in the area of Palestine in *c.* 1208 BC, pointing to the possibility of an Exodus by about 1250 BC (see Documents 10, 11).

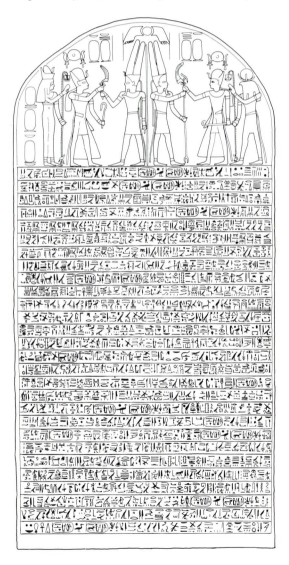

Israel stela of Merneptah (1211–1202 BC) from Thebes; 1208 BC. Granite; ht 318cm. Cairo Museum 34025

Bronze Laver-Stand

This laver-stand belongs to a type of which four nearly complete examples are known. All the examples which have a known provenance are from Cyprus. They have four side panels with open-work relief decoration; the present example has a winged sphinx, a musical scene (illus), a lion, and a horse-drawn chariot. They have four wheels, though another type simply has feet. Most examples support circular collars, usually with some form of decoration.

According to the Book of Kings, one of the items of temple equipment made by the Phoenician craftsman Hiram was what in Hebrew is called a *měkônâ*, 'base' in the Authorised Version, and though the account (1 Kings 7:27-37) presents difficulties of interpretation it appears to describe an object similar to this one. The text states that its purpose was to carry a bronze laver, and the collar on the surviving examples is evidently intended to receive a circular vessel. It is therefore reasonable to render the Hebrew word *měkônâ*, 'laver-stand'. Hiram is said to have made ten of these stands, and to have decorated them with winged sphinxes (*kěrubîm*), lions and bulls, and to have added floral or spiral borders. The dimensions of Hiram's laver-stands are given as about one and a half metres (three cubits) high and about two metres (four cubits) square, very much bigger than the surviving Cypriote examples, the largest of which only stands about forty centimetres high, but the Biblical dimensions are not necessarily to be dismissed.

Bronze, wheeled, laver-stand probably from Cyprus; 13th–11th century BC. Ht 31cm. GR 1946. 10-17.1

Inscribed Arrow-Head

This bronze arrow-head is inscribed in the Phoenician alphabet, 'Arrowhead of 'Ada' son of Ba'l'a'. The word *ḥs* 'arrowhead' is well known in the Old Testament (*ḥēṣ*) where it occurs in parallelism (Is. 5:28; Jer. 50:14; Ezek. 39:3; Ps. 11:2) or coordination (2 Ki. 12:15; Is. 7:24; Ezek. 39:9) with 'bow', and in association (Is.49:2; Ps. 127:4–5) with 'quiver'. There can be little doubt of the meaning of the word *ḥēṣ*, but this rare example of an object which identifies itself as something known in the Hebrew Old Testament illustrates the kind of thing the archaeologist would like to find more often.

This arrowhead, one of twenty now known, also gives evidence of the Phoenician alphabet in the eleventh century BC, the time of the Judges. (See Document 6).

Bronze inscribed arrow-head (front and back), provenance unknown; 11th century BC. Lth 9.1cm. WA 136753

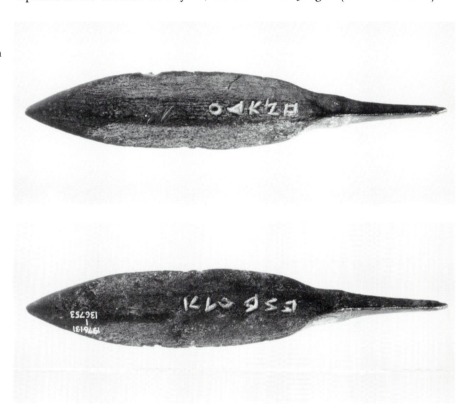

Kurkh Stela of Shalmaneser III

This round-topped stela or monolith, was found at Kurkh on the Tigris in south-eastern Turkey in 1861. It bears a relief carving of king Shalmaneser III of Assyria facing the symbols of four gods, from right to left, Assur, Ishtar, Anu and Sin. Across the front, including the sculpture, and the back of the stela are inscribed 102 lines of cuneiform recording the principal events of his first six military campaigns. In the account of his sixth year, 853 BC (inscribed on the back), he describes his campaign to the west, where he encountered a coalition of states, including Aleppo, Hamath, Aram, Israel and Ammon, at Qarqar on the river Orontes, where he defeated them in battle. The size of each contingent is listed: that of Adad-idri (Biblical Ben-Hadad (2 Ki 6:24; 8:7)) of Damascus consisting of 1200 chariots, 1200 cavalry, and 20,000 infantry; that of Irkhuleni of Hamath 700 chariots, 700 cavalry and 10,000 infantry; and towards the end of line 91 and at the beginning of line 92 on the reverse of the stela (12 and 11 lines from the bottom respectively) the text goes on

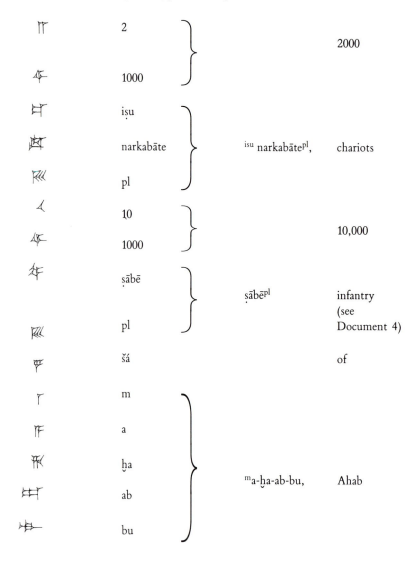

2	}		2000
1000			
iṣu	}	iṣu narkabātepl,	chariots
narkabāte			
pl			
10	}		10,000
1000			
ṣābē	}	ṣābēpl	infantry (see Document 4)
pl			
šá			of
m	}	ma-ḫa-ab-bu,	Ahab
a			
ḫa			
ab			
bu			

𒆳	mātu	
𒅔	sir	
𒀪	'i	^{mātu}sir-'i-la-a-a, the Israelite
𒆷	la	
𒀀	a	
𒀀	a	

The figure of 2000 chariots with 1200 from Damascus and 700 from Hamath is improbably high so a scribal error for 𒐖 , '200' is likely, perhaps under the influence of the frequency of the sign 𒐕 '1000' in this passage. Such errors in the writing of numbers could easily arise when ciphers were used, and this may explain some of the very high numbers in the Old Testament which, though they appear in the Hebrew text as words, probably go back to ciphers in many instances where the Biblical books have been composed with the help of earlier sources.

Stela of Shalmaneser III
(859–824 BC) from Kurkh;
853 BC. Limestone; ht
220cm. WA 118884

45

Black Obelisk of Shalmaneser III

This four-sided stone obelisk, discovered by Layard in 1846, is decorated with five rows of relief sculptures depicting the bringing of tribute to the Assyrian king, each tributary occupying four panels, round the faces of the obelisk, and each identified by a line of script above the scenes. On the stepped top of the obelisk, and on the lower part, also on all four sides, are 190 lines of text describing the principal events of thirty-one military campaigns conducted by Shalmaneser to the Mediterranean in the west, Cilicia in the north-west, Media in the east, and Babylonia and the Gulf in the south. He describes the campaigns against:

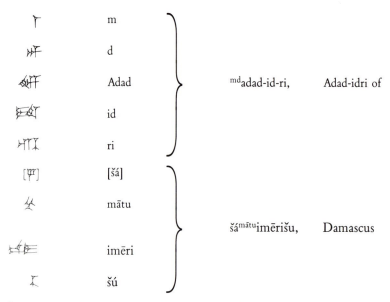

in 853 and 848 BC (see also Document 15) [on Side 4, lines 5–6 of stepped top above reliefs and Side 1, line 16 below reliefs].
and against

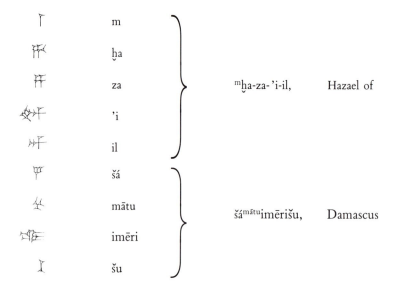

in 841 and 838 BC [on Side 2, lines 2–3 and 8 below reliefs]. Adad-idri appears in the Bible as Ben-Hadad (see Document 15), and Hazail his successor as Hazael (2 Ki. 9:14; 10:32; 12:17; 13:22).

Of particular interest for Biblical Archaeology is the second series (2) of sculptured reliefs, because, though there is no mention of the event in the main text, the caption above these identifies the scenes as representing the Israelite king Jehu bringing tribute to Shalmaneser, an event not mentioned in the Bible.

The Inscription of Side 1 runs:

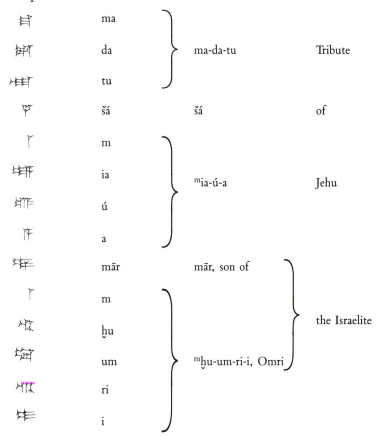

	ma		
	da	ma-da-tu	Tribute
	tu		
	šá	šá	of
	m		
	ia	ᵐia-ú-a	Jehu
	ú		
	a		
	mār	mār, son of	
	m		
	ḫu		the Israelite
	um	ᵐḫu-um-ri-i, Omri	
	ri		
	i		

and continues 'silver, gold, a golden bowl, a golden vase, golden tumblers, golden buckets, tin, a staff for a king, [and] hunting spears, I received'.

The relief scenes show on Side 1 Shalmaneser, below the winged symbol of the Assyrian god Assur, supported by two retainers, receiving the tribute from a dignitary, possibly but not necessarily Jehu himself, who bows to the ground before him.

Jehu was not the son of Omri, and was in fact a usurper of the throne from Omri's descendant Jehoram, but Omri had been such a prominent ruler in his day that the Assyrians referred to Israel as *bit ḫumri*, the 'house of Omri', and it is clear from other Assyrian texts that *mār ḫumri*, literally 'son of Omri' was really only a shorter way of writing *mār bit ḫumri* 'son of the house of Omri' or 'Israelite'.

The other four series of carved scenes are identified by the inscriptions above them as depicting the tribute of, from top to bottom: (1) Sua of Gilzanu; (3) an unnamed

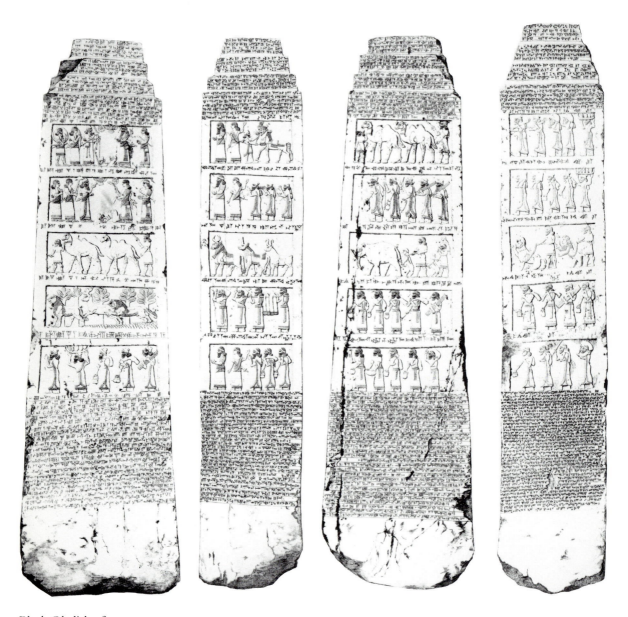

Black Obelisk of
Shalmaneser III (859–824
BC) from Nimrud, ancient
Kalkhu; 841 BC. Ht 198cm.
WA 118885

Detail of side one of Black Obelisk of Shalmaneser III showing the Israelite tribute

ruler of Muṣri; (4) Marduk-apil-uṣur of Sukha; and (5) Qarparunda of Patin. Gilzanu was in Armenia, to the west of Lake Urmia, Muṣri either Egypt or an area in the north Syria-south Asia Minor region, Sukha on the middle Euphrates, and Patin (formerly read Hattin) the Amuq area in north-west Syria. The uncertainty about Muṣri arises from the fact that *muṣri* as a noun means 'borderlands', 'marches' or the like and could therefore be appropriate to more than one place, and though here the tribute described in the text includes a 'river ox', perhaps a hippopotamos, which would point to Egypt, it also mentions and depicts the elephant and the double-humped camel (also depicted in the tribute of Gilzanu) which is distinctly the Bactrian and not the Arabian camel, and therefore points away from Egypt. It is probable that in this present context it is the north Syrian kingdom that is referred to.

The name Muṣri corresponds to Hebrew *miṣrayim* which probably always refers to Egypt in the Old Testament, and is so translated in modern English versions.

Deity in a Fish-Robe

Assyrian bas-relief
showing a deity in a fish
robe from Nimrud; 9th
century BC. Ht 260cm.
WA 124573

This figure is often identified as the Philistine god Dagon on the grounds of a presumed derivation from Hebrew *dag*, 'fish'. Such a suggestion goes back to the Medieval Jewish commentators and influenced the translation of 1 Samuel 5:4, where, describing the fallen statue of Dagon, the Hebrew text reads *raq dāgôn niš'ar 'alāyw*, literally 'only dagon remained on him/it', which does not make sense in the context. To resolve this, various suggestions have been made, one being to reinterpret *dāgôn* as *dāg* ('fish') + *ô* ('his') + *n* (termination) and take it as 'his fish(y part)' or something of the kind. This sort of interpretation lies behind the marginal alternative translation in the Authorised Version 'the fishy' part. There has probably been some corruption in the transmission of the Hebrew text in this passage, so a sure translation is not possible.

When the fish garbed figures, of which this relief is one example, were discovered in Assyria in the last century, they were seen as representations of Dagon on the basis of these ideas. Sir Henry Layard (1817–1894) captioned a reproduction of this example 'Supposed to represent the god Dagon of the Philistines'. In fact, though the three horns on the forehead of the figure show him to have been a god, there is no reason to see him as more than a minor deity, in the same category as the colossal winged, human-headed bulls and lions which guarded the Assyrian palaces. He was possibly associated with Ea (Enki), the god of sweet waters, who is depicted with streams containing fish flowing from his shoulders.

The Dagon of the Philistines was in all probability the Syrian and north Mesopotamian god Dagan who had weather and grain attributes, and indeed the Hebrew word *dāgān*, 'grain, corn' taken over with the Canaanite language, reflects this fact.

Moabite Stone

This black basalt stela bearing a 35 line alphabetic inscription was first seen in 1868 at Dhībān, ancient Dibon, by Reverend F.A. Klein. It was subsequently smashed by local Beduin but a paper squeeze had been taken, and from it a copy of the text was published by T. Nöldeke in 1870, and two large and eighteen smaller surviving fragments were joined together accordingly in the Louvre, which had acquired them in 1873, to produce the restored form of the stela which may now be seen in Paris.

This text begins *'nk mš' bn kmš.. mlk m'b* 'I am Mesha son of Chemosh..., king of Moab', and goes on to say that Omri king of Israel (*'mry mlk yšr'l*) had oppressed Moab for 'many days' and that his son did the same, so Mesha mounted a rebellion, the details of the ensuing war occupying the rest of the inscription.

The war of Israel against Moab is narrated in 2 Kings 3:4–27. Mesha's father is not named, but a fragment of another inscribed stela found in 1958 at El-Kerak in Jordan has made possible its restoration as *kmšyt*, 'Chemoshyat'.

Among the proper names mentioned on the stela, some of them known from the Old Testament, the divine name *yhwh* (see Document no. 41) appears in the statement that Mesha, having captured an Israelite town, 'took from there the vessels of Yahweh and dragged them before Chemosh' (lines 17–18).

Moabite stone from Dhībān, Jordan; 9th century BC. Ht 115cm. Louvre 5066

Astartu Relief of Tiglath-pileser III

Carved stone relief showing Tiglath-pileser III, king of Assyria, 744–727 BC, in his chariot, and above him a fortified city, on a mound or tell, with Assyrian soldiers driving out prisoners and herds. The band of cuneiform across the middle gives part of the text of Tiglath-pileser's Annals and has no direct relation to the reliefs, but above the city is inscribed

	ālu	
	as	ᵃˡᵘas-tar-tu,
	tar	Astartu
	tu	

which gives the name of the defeated city. This is probably Old Testament Ashtaroth in northern Transjordan (Deut. 1:14; Josh. 9:10) a territory which was part of Aram in the period of the Divided Monarchy. The defeat depicted in this relief probably took place during one of the western campaigns of Tiglath-pileser which he conducted in his sixth, eleventh, eighteenth and twenty-first years.

The city is shown on a typical tell, which would have grown up over centuries of building and rebuilding; a process in which the walls of delapidated buildings would have been demolished so that the rooms were filled with rubble – stumps of walls remaining buried – and then the next buildings erected on the levelled remains.

Astartu Relief of Tiglath-pileser III (744–727 BC) from Nimrud; 8th century BC. Ht 188cm. WA 118908

Relief of Sargon II

Sargon succeeded his brother Shalmaneser V as king of Assyria in 721 BC, and though in his annals he appears to claim that he conquered Samaria at the beginning of his reign, it is more likely that it was Shalmaneser V to whom this conquest is to be credited. His invasion and siege are referred to in 2 Kings 17:5; 18:9, and when the conquest is attributed to the 'king of Assyria' in 2 Kings 17:6 and 18:10–11, sometime in 723 or 722 BC, this should be Shalmaneser. When the Assyrians succeeded in conquering a city they consolidated the position by deporting the principal inhabitants. In the case of Samaria the 'king of Assyria', probably Shalmaneser V, is said to have deported Israelites to Syria (river Habur), western Iran (Media) and probably north east Mesopotamia (Ḥalaḥḥu) (2 Ki. 17:6).

Sargon's apparent reference in his annals to the conquest of Samaria may refer to a campaign which he conducted to the west in 720 BC. He claims that he deported 27,280 Israelites to Assyria, and brought in people from other conquered territories to replace them. The Old Testament states that these new settlers, who included some from Cuthah in Babylonia, set up images of their own gods (2 Ki. 17:30–31). These were the ancestors of the Samaritans of the New Testament, people held in contempt by the Jews, whose foreign origins are reflected for instance in the reference to them by Josephus as *Khouthaioi*, 'Cuthaeans' (*Antiquities of the Jews.* XI.88).

Sargon is mentioned only once in the Old Testament, in Isaiah 20:1, where he is said to have sent Tartan (see Document 29) to attack Ashdod, an event which took place in 711 BC.

Relief of Sargon II (721–705 BC) showing him holding a wand and facing one of his officials, from Palace of Sargon at Khorsabad, ancient Dur Sharrukin; 8th century BC. Ht 290cm. WA 118822

Samaria Ivories

These ivories carved in the Phoenician style were found in the royal palace at Samaria, as part of a cache which included winged sphinxes, winged goddesses, scenes of the child Horus seated on a lotus, as well as palmette and lotus patterns. The wings of the sphinxes and other details were enhanced with blue glass inlays, some examples of which are shown at the bottom of the illustration.

These, and other carved ivories from Arslan Tash in Syria, and Nimrud and Khorsabad in Assyria, take the form of boxes, fan handles and similar objects, as well as thin decorated plaques or small carved pieces which could have been decorative elements for furniture.

It is in the light of these that references to ivory in the Old Testament are to be seen. In the tenth century Solomon is said to have made a 'throne [*kissē*'; cf. Document 27] of ivory' (1 Ki. 10:18); in the ninth century mention is made of Ahab's 'ivory house' (1 Ki. 22:39); and in the eighth century the prophet Amos names 'ivory houses' among other luxuries due for divine destruction in Israel (Amos 3:15), and condemns those who lie on 'beds of ivory' (Amos 6:4). The 'ivory houses' would probably simply have been palaces or pavilions furnished with wooden chairs or thrones and beds, decorated with carved ivory, and possibly with ivory panelling on the walls.

When these ivories were discovered at Samaria they were immediately connected with Ahab's 'ivory house', but their archaeological context does not give them any precise date and they could have been deposited in the Palace at any time between its foundation in the early ninth century, and its destruction in 722 BC. The related group found in the Palace of Sargon, to which they had been taken from Phoenicia as booty, make a more precise dating possible because the palace was only built near the end of the eighth century, and even assuming that the ivories were not new at the time, they are unlikely to have been made more than thirty or forty years earlier. This means that the Samaria ivories are probably to be dated to the eighth century, and that the references in the Book of Amos are the closest in date. Nevertheless, ivory carving had been practiced in the Near East since the second millennium BC, and indeed a fine group of the twelfth century BC was discovered at Megiddo, so there is no reason to think that Solomon and Ahab did not have decorative ivories, only that tenth and ninth century examples have not yet been found.

Ivories from Samaria; 8th century BC. WA L 31–48 (PEF 1–18)

Royal Stamped Jar Handles

These handles of pottery jars which had been stamped, before baking, with seals show symbols, either a four-winged scarab or a two-winged disc, with *lmlk*, 'belonging to the king' written above it in Hebrew script and a place-name below it. Over eight hundred of these stamped handles have been found at over twenty excavated sites in Palestine, nearly all in the territory to which Judah was confined by about 700 BC. The place names are:

		English Bible	Modern
ꜩꜹꝗꟈ	ḥbrn	Hebron (Gen. 13:18; Josh. 10:3; 2 Sam. 15: 10 etc.)	el-Khalil
ꝗꞩ	zp	Ziph (Josh. 15:24; 1 Sam. 23:14–15, 24, etc)	Tell Zif
ꟼꝆꝘꟉ	šwkh	Socoh (Josh. 15:35; 1 Sam. 17:1; 1 Ki 4:10)	Khirbet 'Abbad
ꝿꞩ ꟉꝆ	mmšt		

Royal stamped jar handles from Tell ed-Duweir, ancient Lachish; late 8th century BC. *From left to right* WA 132061 (zp), 132065 (ḥbrn), 160142 (šwkh), 160317 (mmšt)

The fourth name does not occur in the Bible and its identity has been much discussed. The most promising theory would identify it with Emmaus, modern Amwas, the name of which can be plausibly connected with *mmšt*. If this identification is accepted, and the four places are taken to be administrative centres, they are found to lie quite suitably in four districts, each made up of three of the twelve administrative areas known from earlier Biblical texts such as Joshua 15:20–62. According to this, Socoh and Hebron fall respectively within a west and an east central district, Ziph within a southern and Emmaus within a northern district. Stamped handles with all four place names have been found throughout Judah, so a possible explanation would be that the products contained in the store jars to which these are the handles were first collected at the four provincial administrative centres, then passed in bulk to Jerusalem, and were then redistributed from there.

Most of the surviving stamped handles are broken away from the original jars, but a small number of jars have been reconstructed and these show that they stood abut two feet in height, and had a capacity of between nine and ten gallons.

The archaeological contexts of these handles will only date them to a time in the eighth or seventh centuries BC. Though they cannot be positively connected with any particular king, a strong possibility is that Hezekiah was the ruler in question. The vessels would have been suitable for any of the three staples derived from the land, grain, wine or oil, and indeed these, in their unprocessed state, are listed among his wealth (2 Chron. 32:28).

Assyrian Tribute List

This small cuneiform tablet, undated, but probably of the time of Sargon II or Sennacherib, listing tribute from Ammon (two manus of gold), Moab (one manu of gold), Judah (ten manus of silver), Edom and Byblos (quantities destroyed). The Babylonian *manu*, made up of sixty *šiqlu*, weighed about 505 gm., similar to the Hebrew *māneh*, used to weigh gold (1 Ki. 10:11) and silver (Ezra 2:69; Neh. 7:71, 72), which was made up of fifty *šeqel*, which weighed about 500 gm. (e.g. 2 Sam. 14.26).

Assyrian Tribute List
from Kuyunjik, ancient
Nineveh; 8th–7th century
BC. Baked clay; ht 4.4cm.
WA K 1295

Assyrian Scale Armour

This group of bronze scales, stuck together as a result of corrosion in the ground, represents a type of armour well known in the Near East. Examples of the Late Bronze Age, fifteenth to thirteenth centuries BC, are known from Asia Minor, Persia, north Mesopotamia, Syria, Palestine, and Egypt.

The present examples, later representatives of the same tradition, were found with a mass of others, many of them of iron, in a store room, presumably the armourer's store, at Fort Shalmaneser, Nimrud. Also in the room were found pottery jars which seem to have contained olive oil, perhaps for lubricating the armour. The Assyrian examples of armour scales appear most commonly to have been laced together, through specially located holes, so that they would over lap to form a flexible garment. They were less often sewn to a cloth or leather backing.

Scale armour is mentioned in the Old Testament where, in the description of the armour of Goliath the Philistine giant, the word *širyôn*, 'armour' is qualified as *qaśqaśśîm* (1 Sam. 17:5), and *qaśqaśśîm* is used in a passage in Deuteronomy which distinguishes clean from unclean foods to describe the scales of a fish (Deut. 14:9). There can be little doubt therefore that this passage is saying that Goliath was dressed in scale armour.

The present example is, of course, of later date than the time appropriate to David and Goliath, eleventh to tenth century BC, but Late Bronze Age examples from Megiddo, Lachish and Tell el-Ajjul (probably Beth Eglayim), show the type was in use before that time in Palestine.

Assyrian scale armour from Nimrud; 7th century BC. Bronze; lth of scale 6.3cm. WA 132699

Royal Steward Inscription

This inscription, discovered in 1870 by C. Clermont Ganneau, was not fully deciphered until 1953 by N. Avigad, largely because its extremely rough surface made the characters very difficult to see. They have been marked with white pigment to make them more legible. It was located as the lintel to a rock-cut tomb, and refers to the burial. The script may be dated in the seventh century BC, and the language is standard Hebrew. It begins (top line from right to left):

	z't	this	This is
	...		[the tomb of]
	...yhw	...iah	...iah
	'šr	who	
	'l	over	the Royal Steward
	hbyt	the house	

and goes on to say that there is no silver or gold there, only his bones and the bones of his maid servant, and concludes by cursing any man who opens it. The phrase *'šr 'l hbyt* is known from the Old Testament as the designation of an official whose post seemed to increase in importance over the centuries, first applying to a sort of palace administrator (1 Ki. 4:6; 16:9), then to an officer with political responsibilities (1 Ki. 18:3–4), and by the seventh century to the senior minister of the kingdom (2 Ki. 10:5; 15:5; 18:18; 19:2). The official bearing this title in the time of Hezekiah, Shebna, was berated by Isaiah for carving himself a tomb in the rocky hillside (Is. 22:15–25), and this has led to the quite plausible speculation that the present inscription comes from the tomb of Shebna. The name of the owner is partly destroyed, and what survives, the divine ending *-yhw*, '-iah', does not correspond to the form of the name given in Isaiah, which is *šebna'*, but the form *šĕbanyāhû*, which does occur in Nehemiah (9:4), is generally recognised as a fuller form of the same name, so the identity of the two, and therefore the attribution of this inscription to Shebna, or Shebniah, the Royal Steward of Hezekiah, is a distinct possibility.

Royal Steward Inscription from Silwan, near Jerusalem; 7th century BC. Limestone; lth 221cm. WA 125205

Annals of Sennacherib

Annals of Sennacherib
(Taylor Prism) from
Kuyunjik (691–689 BC).
Baked clay; ht 38.5cm.
WA 91032

Six sided clay prism inscribed with an account of the first eight military campaigns of Sennacherib, king of Assyria 705–681 BC. It was found at Nebi Yunus (Ninevah) by Colonel R. Taylor in 1830. Much the same text is preserved on a prism (the Chicago Prism) in the University of Chicago.

In the account of his third campaign, which took place in 701 BC, Sennacherib describes his march to the west, where he defeated the Phoenicians, notably at Tyre and Sidon, and his move southwards, where he received tribute from Pudu-ilu of Ammon, Kammusunadbi of Moab, and Aiarammu of Edom, all in Transjordan. In Philistia Mitinti of Ashdod payed tribute, but Sidqa of Ashkelon was rebellious so Sennacherib replaced him with Sharruludari.

According to the Annals, Sennacherib now encountered an Egyptian army which was coming to the aid of the inhabitants of Palestine. The Egyptian commander is not named in the Annals, but parallel Biblical accounts identify him as Tirhaqa (2 Ki. 19:19; Is. 37:9), Taharqa in the Egyptian sources, a Nubian who ruled as Pharaoh from about 690–664 BC. Though Sennacherib's invasion took place some ten years before Taharqa became king, he was probably about twenty years old at the time and could have been in titular command of the Egyptian army. The Biblical description of him as 'king of Nubia (*kŭs*)' could simply reflect an edition of the text dating from a time after he became king.

The best known passage in this description states that because Hezekiah (*ḫa-za-qi-a-u*) had not submitted to the Assyrian 'yoke', Sennacherib laid siege to forty-six fortified Judaean cities, deported 200,150 people, and invested Hezekiah in Jerusalem. This event is described from the other point of view in 2 Kings 18:17–19:36 and Isaiah 36:1–37:37) where three Assyrian officials, the Tartan (see Document 29), the Rabsaris (see Document 30) and the Rabshaqeh (see Document 29), are described as coming to the city. According to the Biblical account the Rabshaqeh shouted to the defenders, represented on the walls by three high officials Eliaqim, Shebna and Joah, in Hebrew rather than Aramaic ('Syrian' in AV and RV), which was by then a lingua franca in the Near East, calling on them to surrender. Hezekiah refused both on this occasion and subsequently when the Rab-shaqeh returned after consultation with sennacherib at Lachish.

The Biblical account concludes with the much debated statement that the Assyrian army was struck down in some way during the night with considerable loss of life, following which the siege was called off (2 Ki. 19:35-36; Is. 27:36–37). The Assyrian Annals tacitly agree with the Biblical version by making no claim that Jerusalem was taken, only describing tribute from Hezekiah of gold, silver, precious stones, valuable woods, furniture decorated with ivory (cf. Document 21), iron daggers, raw iron, and musicians (cf. 2 Ki. 18:13–16).

This prism inscription is rich in information, but no mention is made of the siege of Lachish which took place during the same campaign and which is illustrated by the famous series of reliefs in the British Museum (Document 27).

Siege of Lachish Reliefs

The second book of Chronicles states that when Sennacherib invaded Palestine (in 701 BC) he established his headquarters in front of Lachish and that he dispatched his senior officers to Jerusalem from there (2 Chron. 32:9). Neither the Old Testament nor his own annals (see Document 26) say more about the fate of Lachish, but the long series of reliefs from his Palace at Nineveh illustrate what happened to it.

The Assyrian troops are shown advancing from the left. The city is attacked with wheeled, armoured, battering rams onto which one soldier is pouring water against burning brands thrown down by the defenders. To the right the defeated inhabitants are led out by Assyrian troops, some of whom carry braziers or incense stands, perhaps from unorthodox religious rites. Further along, Sennacherib is shown on a throne in front of his camp receiving the capitulation from an official. Some of the upper details on the slabs are lost as a result of damage to the reliefs when the Palace of Sennacherib was destroyed in 612 BC.

Below and following page
Siege of Lachish Reliefs
from Kuyunjik; 701 BC.
Ht *c.* 250cm; lth *c.* 18.9m.
WA 124902–15

The whole sequence is identified by an inscription over the figure of Sennacherib which runs:

1		m			
		d			
		sin	ᵐᵈsîn-aḫḫē-eriba	Sennacherib
		aḫḫē			
		eriba			
		šar	šar	king of
		kiššati	kiššati	the world
		šar	šar	king of
		mātu	ᵐᵃᵗᵘaššur	Assyria
		aššur			

continued overleaf

0 cm.

61

2	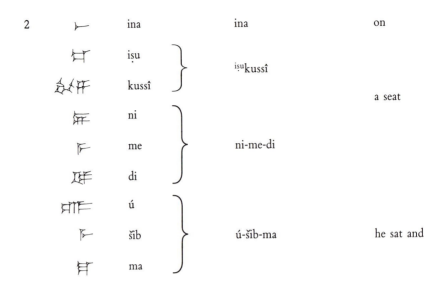 ina	ina	on
	iṣu		
	kussî	iṣukussî	
			a seat
	ni		
	me	ni-me-di	
	di		
	ú		
	šib	ú-šib-ma	he sat and
	ma		

3		šal			
		la	}	šal-la-at	the booty of
		at			
		ālu	}	ᵃˡᵘla-ki-su	Lachish
		la			
		ki			
		su			

continued overleaf

0   50   100 cm.

Detail showing
Sennacherib receiving the
capitulation of the city

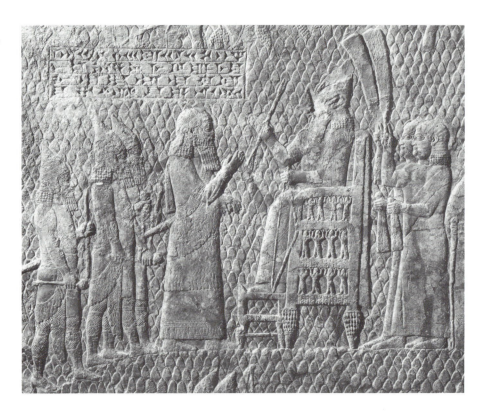

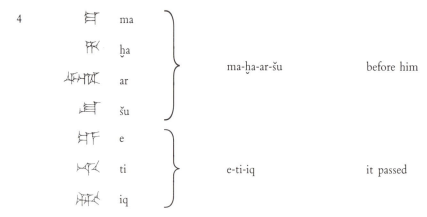

4		ma			
		ḫa			
		ar	}	ma-ḫa-ar-šu	before him
		šu			
		e			
		ti	}	e-ti-iq	it passed
		iq			

In this passage it is worth noting some of the Hebrew cognates to the vocabulary: *šarru*, 'king' with Hebrew *śar*, 'chief, ruler, captain, prince'; *iṣu* 'wood' (here a determinative which was not pronounced), with *'ēṣ* 'tree, wood'; *kussu* 'seat', with *kisse'*, 'throne' (see Document 21); *ušib* 'he sat', from *ašābu* 'to sit', with *yāšab*, 'to sit'. This is typical of the Assyrian inscriptions and illustrates their value to the modern scholar for refining and defining the Hebrew vocabulary.

Vassal Treaty of Esarhaddon

Vassal Treaty of
Esarhaddon (680–669 BC)
from Nimrud, 672 BC.
Baked clay; ht 28cm.
WA 132548

This represents a treaty between Esarhaddon, king of Assyria, 680–669 BC, and some of his vassals. The king organised a ceremonial gathering of his vassals at Kalkhu (Biblical Calah), modern Nimrud, in 672 BC to ensure their loyalty to his heir Ashurbanipal, and the text lays down the treaty conditions which he imposed by him. Each vassal received a copy of the treaty, and fragments of nine copies were found in the excavations at Nimrud. The version in the British Museum is very fragmentary, but there is a much more complete version in the Iraq Museum, Baghdad, and enough fragments survive to make possible the restoration of much of the text. The vassals mentioned in these versions were situated to the east and south-east of Assyria, but this is the kind of treaty what would have been imposed by the Assyrians on the kingdoms of Israel and Judah. The contemporary ruler of Judah, Manasseh, is unlikely to have been in Kalkhu for the ceremony of 672 BC, because he was involved in an attempt by several western states to break away from Assyrian rule in 674 BC, and this move was not quelled by Esarhaddon until 671 BC. Manasseh is however mentioned in Esarhaddon's annals (written *me-na-si-i* and *mi-in-si-e*) as a tributary some time between 671 and 669 BC.

The interest of this treaty goes further back, however, because in form it partially follows a literary pattern now recognised in several other documents. This pattern is found not only in rediscovered ancient treaties but also in the Bible in the agreements referred to in Authorised Version English as 'covenants'. According to it, the document begins with a Preamble or Title; this is followed by a Historical account of past relations between the parties; then come the Provisions of the treaty, that is to say, what is expected of each of the parties; there is often mention of the Placing of a copy of the treaty in the vassal's sanctuary and arrangements for periodic Reading of the provisions; a list of Witnessing gods comes next; and there is a concluding section of Curses and Blessings for the degree of fullfillment of the provisions. The Hebrew word *bĕrît* which is commonly translated 'covenant' can quite reasonably be rendered 'treaty' or something of the kind, and the main elements can be seen in such 'covenants' as that set out in Exodus 20–31; Deuteronomy 1–32 and Joshua 24. It has been noted that in the ancient treaties a difference is found between those of the latter part of the second millenium BC, which contain most of the elements outlined above, and those of the first millenium BC, like the Esarhaddon vassal treaty, which vary somewhat in the sequence, and indeed do not always include all of the elements. In this respect the Biblical convenants in Exodus, and Deuteronomy conform more to the usage of the late second millennium than that of the first.

Assyrian Eponym List

The fragment of a tablet giving a list of the Assyrian Limmus or eponyms for the years 858–847 BC, further years which were originally on the tablet having been broken away. The Assyrians named their years after high officials in cycles, beginning with the king, each office holder was designated Limmu for the year in question.

The present tablet sets the information out in four columns, the first, here largely broken away, reading 'in the Limmuship of', the second giving the name of the official, the third his rank, and the fourth, here again largely broken away, giving a principal event of the year in question.

The first line, separated from what follows by a horizontal ruling, is damaged at the beginning and end, but (with restoration in brackets) reads '[Reign] of Shalmaneser son of Ashurnasirpal...' referring to Shalmaneser III (858–824 BC). (See also Documents 15, 16). Shalmaneser was Limmu for the first time in 857 BC, and this is listed in the second line below the ruling, where he appears as 'Shalmaneser, king of Assyria'. The two following lines, for the years 856 and 855 BC, indicate that the Limmuship was next held by the men designated respectively (in the right hand column)

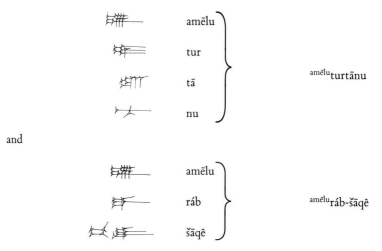

and

According to the Old Testament, the holders of these two offices in 701 BC appeared, together with the Rabsaris (see Document 30), before the walls of Jerusalem, in local command of the army of Sennacherib (2 Ki. 18:17; see Document 26).

Assyrian Eponym List from Kuyunjik; 7th century BC. Baked clay; ht 5.7cm. WA 82–5–22, 526

Bilingual Clay Label

A clay label probably from a bale bound with cords, the impressions of which remain in the centre. It is inscribed on one side in Assyrian cuneiform with an account of barley issued to an individual named Handuate, and on the other with a summary in alphabetic Aramaic. The quantity involved is given on the Assyrian side as five *imēru* for seven months. The *imēru* was an ass-load, something like 13.5 litres, the volume involved here therefore being about 67.5 litres, a considerable quantity, implying a very large bale. The Hebrew counterpart of the *imēru* was the *homer*, defined for instance in Ezekiel 45:11 as ten ephahs or 'baths', and shown to be a substantial quantity by the statement in Leviticus 27:16 that a homer of barley was worth fifty shekels (or about 570 grammes) of silver.

This label is dated to the year when Nabu-shar-usur was Limmu (682 BC). The Aramaic text concluded *l'm rbsrs nbsrṣr*, 'Limmu of Rabsaris Nabu-šar-uṣur'. The term Rabsaris was the title of an Assyrian high official, the Aramaic form *rbsrs* being a loan-word from Assyrian *rab ša rēši* 'chief of the head' or something of the kind, indicating a man close to the king, and therefore of importance. The title appears in the consonantal spelling *rbsrys* in 2 Kings 18:17 where this officer and two others, Tartan and Rabshakeh (see Document 29), are described as having been sent by Sennacherib from his camp at Lachish to lay siege to Hezekiah in Jerusalem (see Document 26).

Bilingual clay label from Kuyunjik; 682 BC. Lth 5.2cm. WA 81–2–4, 147

A 'Letter to God'

This tablet, the middle part of the original text, is itself made up of three fragments whose connection was only recognised in 1973. It describes the campaign of an Assyrian king, whose name is missing, against Judah, and twice mentions the name of the Judaean king, only partially preserved on each occasion, as '...iah' (*...ia-a-u mātu ia-u-da-a-a*) and speaks of the capture of the city of Azekah and of a Philistine city, of which the name is lost, but which had been captured and fortified previously by '...iah'. The identity of the Judaean king is uncertain. There were three with names ending with the divine element '-iah' (*-yāhu*) who reigned during the time of the Assyrian westward expansion, namely Amaziah in the time of Adad-nirari III, Uzziah (Azariah) in the time of Tiglath-pileser III and Hezekiah in the time of Sargon and Sennacherib. Of these, only Uzziah and Hezekiah are credited in the Old Testament with conquests in Philistia (2 Chron 26:6; 2 Ki 18:8), but neither of them satisfactorily fits the historical circumstances and the damaged spaces available for the restoration of the names.

The identification of both the Judaean and Assyrian kings must therefore remain open, and this document illustrates the tantalising nature of some evidence of significance for Biblical Archaeology. This document also illustrates another aspect of the development of Near Eastern and Biblical studies. It is made up of three fragments, the right hand one (K.6205) having been published in 1870 as a document of the time of Tiglath-pileser III, and the two left hand fragments in 1958 as of the time of Sargon. The right hand fragment which mentions '...iah of Judah', was incorrectly incorporated in a reconstruction of the Annals of Tiglath-pileser III published in 1893. This led to the assumption that a ruler who appears elsewhere in the Annals, Azriyau (*az-ri-ia-a-u*), the name of whose state is not otherwise recorded, was Uzziah (Azariah) of Judah. The recognition that the fragment in question had nothing to do with Tiglath-pileser has led to the conclusion that Azriyau was an otherwise unknown north Syrian ruler. This revision will gradually work its way into the standard history textbooks, illustrating a continuing process.

Clay tablet from Kuyunjik; 7th century BC. Ht 7.5cm. WA K 6205+82–3–23, 131

Creation Epic

The story of creation in the Bible forms the first part of Genesis, and the best known Mesopotamian account is that found in the composition known to the Assyrians as *enuma eliš* ('when above') from its first two words. This was by no means the only Mesopotamian composition which described creation, for instance, the Epic of Atrahasis (Document 3) also contained an account, but since it was the first cuneiform text dealing with the subject which the early decipherers worked on, it gained a public interest which it has retained in the popular literature. It is typical of the genre. It was copied on seven tablets from earlier sources in the time of Ashurbanipal in the seventh century BC. It begins by saying that 'when above' the heaven and below the earth had no name and there was no land, the primeval gods Apsu and Tiamat procreated the other gods. In due course, Tiamat regretted the creation of these gods and she produced a brood of monsters to destroy them. The gods chose Marduk to deal with this problem, which he did effectively, ending by cleaving Tiamat in two, the halves forming the heavens above and the earth and underworld below. This account is typical of others and shows that, apart from individual details, the Mesopotamian creation stories have little in common with the early chapters of Genesis.

Creation epic (Enuma eliš) from Kuyunjik; 7th century BC. Baked clay; ht 80cm. WA K 5419+

Gilgamesh Epic

One of the great literary compositions of ancient Mesopotamia was the Epic of Gilgamesh, mainly known from copies of the seventh century BC found at Nineveh. The main theme is the search by the hero Gilgamesh for immortality. The author or authors, of the basic version who may have lived sometime in the eighteenth or seventeenth century BC, made use of existing literary material which he or they knitted together into a unified composition. The epic occupies eleven tablets (a twelfth in the Assyrian version is probably a later edition). The eleventh tablet contains the story told to Gilgamesh by Utnapishtim, a hero living in a distant land, of how he gained immortality. He narrates how the gods became angry at the nuisance caused on the earth by men and decided to destroy them with a flood. Utnapishtim was specially favoured by the god Ea, who warned him to build a ship and to bring into it all his family, his treasures, and living creatures of every kind. He does this and so escapes a prodigious storm leading to a flood which destroys all the rest of mankind. The storm ends on the seventh day, and on the twelfth day land emerges from the waters. In due course the boat comes to rest on Mount Nisir (in Kurdistan) and Utnapishtim sends out in turn a dove, a swallow and a raven, only the raven not returning. Finally Utnapishtim emerges from the boat, and offers a sacrifice to the gods.

This version, which made a tremendous stir in Victorian England when George Smith announced its discovery in 1872, supplies details about the resting place of the boat and the episode of the birds, which are missing in the Atrahasis Epic (Document 3). It is likely, however, that the author made use of the Atrahasis Epic in compiling his work and these elements probably formed part of the damaged third tablet of that composition.

Gilgamesh Epic, Tablet XI, from Kuyunjik; 7th century BC. Baked clay; ht 15.5cm. WA K 3375

Moabite Seal

Moabite dome-backed
stamp Seal from Ur,
Babylonia; 7th century BC.
Lapis lazuli; diam. 1cm.
WA 116598

This small circular lapis lazuli seal is inscribed *kmš ntn*, 'Chemosh-nathan', the name
of the owner. As a name it follows exactly the same pattern as *yhw ntn* 'Jonathan' where
the first element is the name of a god, and the second the verb 'he has given'. Jonathan
probably means 'Yahweh has given (a son)' and Chemosh-nathan 'Chemosh has given
(a son)'. Just as Yahweh was the God of the Hebrews, Chemosh (or Kemosh), as is
shown by the Old Testament (Nu. 21:29; Jer. 48:46), was the god of the Moabites.

This seal was excavated at Ur by Sir Leonard Woolley (1880–1960) and its presence
could suggest that the owner was living there, though whether as a merchant or a
deportee or the descendant of a deportee is not clear, since no Moabite deportations
are mentioned among the many recorded in the cuneiform records.

Philistine Seal

Philistine scaraboid Seal
found in Dundrum,
Ireland; 7th century BC.
Agate; lth 2.7cm. WA 48502

This scaraboid seal bears the alphabetic inscription

ग≮≺⟊ᴲᵍᴑᴸ	l'bd'l'b	To 'Abd'eli'ab
ᴲᴈ	bn	son of
✕ᴅᴈᴡ	š'bt	Shib'at
⟊ᴈᴑ	'bd	retainer (literally 'servant') of
✕✕ᴵᴴ	mtt	Mitinti
ᴴᴈ	bn	son of
≮ᴘᴿᴵᴸ	ṣdq'	Ṣidqa

In this, the name *mtt* is interpreted as 'Mitinti' because the Assyrian king Esarhaddon (680–699 BC) in describing a western campaign in his Annals in about 670 BC, lists a Mitinti of Ashkelon among those who paid tribute to him, while Sennacherib mentions that during the campaign in which he attacked Lachish (Document 27) and Jerusalem (Document 26), in 701 BC he replaced Ṣidqa, the rebellious ruler of Ashkelon. The Assyrian Annals do not identify Mitinti as the son of Ṣidqa, but the text on this seal makes it a reasonable assumption, and illustrates the contribution which so small an object can make to the reconstruction of history.

Others who paid tribute to Esarhaddon at the same time as Mitinti included the rulers of Ammon, Moab, Edom, Ekron, Ashdod, Gaza, and the ruler of Judah whose name, written *me-na-si-i*, was clearly Manasseh. This tribute from Manasseh to Esarhaddon is mentioned not in the Old Testament where Esarhaddon only appears, in effect, twice: once in reference to the death of Sennacherib and his succession to the throne (2 Kings 19:37 = Is. 37:38); and once in connection with his settlement of deportees in Samaria (Ezra 4:2).

When this seal came to light in Ireland in the mid-nineteenth century, it was taken as Phoenician and gave rise to speculation about Phoenician trade with the British Isles, but the possibilities of its having been dropped there perhaps in Roman times or in the eighteenth century are more plausible.

Iron-Age Tomb Group

This group of pottery vessels is typical of the period of the Divided Monarchy in Palestine. When Jeremiah used the metaphor of the potter to clarify his prophetic message (Jer. 18: 1–12) it was just such vessels as these that he might have had in mind. The bronze rings, probably anklets or bracelets, suggest that this was the tomb of a woman. The pottery figurine, which depicts a woman supporting her breasts with her hands, is clearly a fertility figurine, and is not the sort of thing that could have been in the hands of any faithful worshipper of Yahweh (see Document 41). The prophets condemned the Israelites for whoring after other gods (Hos. 9:1; Ezek. 6:9; 23:30), and the occupant of this tomb was clearly such a heretic. Many other examples of this type of figurine found in excavations, show that this was a widespread phenomenon.

Iron Age Tomb Group from near Bethlehem; *c.* 7th century BC. WA 48288–96, 93091, 102755

Paym Weight

Paym Weight from Tell ed-Duweir, ancient Lachish; 7th–6th century BC. Yellow limestone; diam 1.35cm; wt 7.805gm. WA 160316

This weight of yellow limestone, a sphere with a flattened base, is of a type known from a number of excavated sites in Palestine, and, since the average weight of these examples is 7.82 gm, it could be interpreted as two-thirds of a 'common' shekel of about 11.73 gm.

The inscription on it simply gives the Hebrew consonants *pym* (from right to left) and this spelling, vocalised *pîm* in the Old Testament, is found in a passage in 1 Samuel which describes the Philistine monopoly of metalworking in Palestine in the time of Saul. According to the text there was no smith in Israel, and the Israelites went to the Philistines to have their tools sharpened. The charge was a *pîm* for the ploughshares, the axes, the three(-tined) forks, the adzes and the setting of the goads (1 Sam. 13: 19–21). The *pîm* here presumably represented that weight in silver.

Until *pym* weights were found in excavations, translators had difficulty in understanding the above quoted passage, and it still presents some difficulty because of uncertainty about another word (*pĕṣîrâ*) in it. Various versions differ in their translations of some of the implements mentioned but, apart from this, the difficult passage is

Hebrew	AV/RV	Literally
wĕhāyĕta	Yet they had	And it was
happĕṣîrâ	a file	the *pĕṣîrâ*
pîm	['for the mouth' (RV margin)]	*paym*
lammahărēṣōt	for the mattocks	for the ploughshares
etc.		

The Authorised Version translation was retained by the Revised Version (1885) since the first *pym* weight did not come to light until 1903 (a bronze cube purchased in Jerusalem) and the first known example of the sub-spherical stone type was only excavated in 1907 at Gezer.

While Hebrew *pîm*, probably to be vocalised *paym* (a dual), 'two mouths' or 'two parts', shows the general intention of the passage, *pĕṣîrâ* which occurs only this once in the Old Testament, has no clear explanation, though the context suggests some such meaning as 'imposed charge', or 'fixed price', which is possible etymologically. The New English Bible assumes such an interpretation in translating 'The charge was two-thirds of a shekel for ploughshares....'.

Beqa' Weight

A dome shaped stone weight of pink limestone inscribed in Hebrew *bq'* literally 'divided'. Exodus 38:26 defines the 'bekah' as 'half a sheqel', according to the standard referred to as the 'sheqel of the sanctuary'. The average weight of the known examples, 6.115 gm, would give a sheqel on this standard of about 12.20 gm.

The word also occurs in the account of the finding of Rebecca as a bride for Isaac. Abraham sent his senior servant to northern Mesopotamia where he encountered Rebecca at a well and offered her a gold earring weighing a *beqa'*, as well as two gold bracelets weighing ten sheqels, to introduce himself to her father's house (Gen. 24:22).

Beqa' Weight from Tell ed-Duweir, ancient Lachish; 7th–6th century BC. Pink limestone; ht 1.55cm; wt 6.095gm. WA 132828

Hannaniah Sealing

A small lump of clay with the impression of a seal inscribed

𐤋𐤇𐤍𐤍𐤉𐤄𐤅	lḥ nnyhw	Belonging to Hannaniah
𐤁𐤍	bn	son of
𐤂𐤃𐤋𐤉𐤄𐤅	gdlyhw	Gedaliah

and showing the impression of papyrus and thread on the back.

The two names, which are identified as Hebrew by the ending *-yhw* (-iah), an abbreviated form of the divine name Yahweh (see Document 41). are both born by several individuals in the Old Testament. Gedaliah was, of course, the name of the ruler left by Nebuchadnezzar in Jerusalem in 586 BC (2 Ki. 25:22). He was descended from a line of state officials (cf. 2 Ki 22:3–20; 2 Ch. 34:14–28) having no connection with the royal family of Judah. It is possible, but by no means certain, that the seal which made this impression was that of the son an otherwise unknown Gedaliah.

The surface on the back of this lump shows that it was used to seal a rolled-up papyrus document. References in the Old Testament to inscribed scrolls (Ps. 40:8; Jer. 36:2–4; Ezek. 2:9) suggest that these were papyrus rather than leather. The episode in which Jehioaqim has the written prophecy of Jeremiah burnt piece by piece in his brazier strongly suggests that the material was papyrus (Jer. 36:20–25).

Clay sealing, probably from Palestine; 6th century BC. Lth 1.1cm. WA 134695

Brick of Nebuchadnezzar

The rulers in ancient Mesopotamia had bricks inscribed with their names to use in important buildings, and though the inscriptions could not be seen while the building was standing, they would identify the work to later restorers, and provide valuable evidence for modern archaeologists.

This example is inscribed in an archaising cuneiform script, 'Nebuchadnezzar, King of Babylon, preserver of Esagila and Ezida, eldest son of Nabopolassar, King of Babylon', Esagila and Ezida being temples in Babylon.

The brick has also been inscribed *zbn'* in Aramaic script. This is a personal name of a Jew, known in the Bible as Zebina (*zbn'*), who was among those who had married foreign wives in the time of Ezra (Ezra 10:43). It is found also in the cuneiform sources, among others in the business archives of the trading house of Murashu which flourished at Nippur in Neo-Babylonian times and which had dealings with many of the Jews in exile. The name *za-bi-na-a'* occurs fives times in the surviving Murashu documents, probably referring to more than one individual. The father and son of one of these five are given as Tobiah (*tu-ub-ia-a-ma*) and Baaliah (*ba-li-ia-a-ma*) respectively, the termination *-ia-a-ma*, corresponding at that time to Hebrew *-yahu*, the divine element Yahweh, showing clearly that in that instance at least Zabina' was a Jew.

Brick of Nebuchadnezzar
from Babylonia; 6th
century BC. Ht 35cm.
WA 90136

Lachish Ostracon

One of a group of ostraca (pot sherds) inscribed in ink in alphabetic Hebrew, which were found in or near the main gate of ancient Lachish (modern Tell ed-Duweir) in a burnt layer associated with the destruction of the city in 586 BC (level II). This was the time when the Babylonians under Nebuchadnezzar had invaded Judah and were besieging Zedekiah, Nebuchadnezzar's own rebellious appointee, in Jerusalem. According to Jeremiah, apart from Jerusalem, only Azekah, about eighteen miles south-west of Jerusalem, and Lachish, about twelve miles further, remained in Judaean hands as the invasion progressed. The ostraca belong to this time, and are mostly letters written from outposts to a man named Ya'osh, the military commander at Lachish, reporting on the situation. Most of them use the language of polite formality, rather unexpectedly in view of the critical situation which culminated in total defeat.

The present example begins

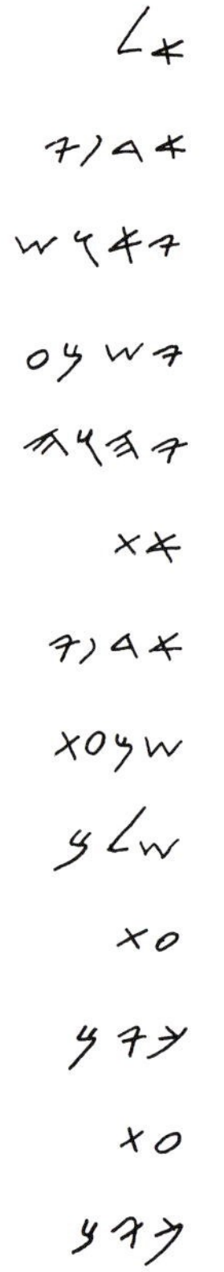

l.1		'l	To
		'dny	my lord
		y'wš	Ya'osh
		yšm'	May he cause to hear
l.2		yhwh	Yahweh
		't	
		'dny	my lord
		š[m't]	news of
ll.2/3		šlm	peace
		't	time
		kym	now
		't	time
		kym	now

May Yahweh cause my lord to hear news of peace, even now, even now.

78

Lachish Ostracon from Tell ed-Duweir; 586 BC. Baked clay; ht 9cm. WA 125702

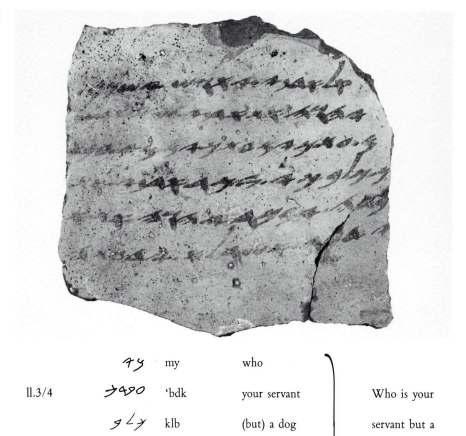

	my	who	Who is your
ll.3/4	'bdk	your servant	servant but a
	klb	(but) a dog	dog that my
	ky	that	lord should
	zkr	should remember	remember his
	'dny	my lord	servant?
l.45	't ['bdh	his servant	

There are several points to note in this passage. In vocabulary and grammar it is virtually indistinguishable from the Hebrew of the Old Testament. The divine name *yhwh*, is that of the God of the Old Testament where the consonants *yhwh* are written with the vowels *-e-ō-ā-*, leading to the familiar form Yehōwāh, or, as Tyndale and his successors wrote it, Jehovah. What they did not realise however was that the vowels were intended to remind the reader in a Synagogue that he should speak the word *'adōnāy* 'my lord', since the divine name was too holy to pronounce (the *e* became *a* after the consonant'). The form Yahweh is based on Greek spellings in the writings of the early Christian Fathers. The passage 'who is your servant but a dog, that my lord should remember his servant' is fairly closely echoed in 2 Kings 8:13, which includes the phrase *mh 'bdk hklb ky*, 'what is your servant, the dog, that...?' More distant echoes of this mode of speech are found in 2 Sam. 9:8 and 16:9.

Cylinder Inscription of Nabonidus

This cylinder, one of four bearing the same text found at the four corners of the ziggurat (*ziq-qur-rat*) at Ur, is inscribed in Babylonian cuneiform with an account of its rebuilding by Nabonidus. The inscription records that he learned from early inscriptions that the ziggurat had been begun by Ur-Nammu and completed by Shulgi, kings of the Third Dynasty of Ur some 1500 years earlier (see Document 2). Nabonidus says that he reconstructed it on its old foundations and concludes the inscription with a prayer to the moon god Sin to whom the ziggurat was consecrated. This prayer is of particular interest since it ends (right hand column, lines 24–6) with a plea for the piety of

l.24		m		
		^{d}bēl		
		šar	^{md}bēl-šar-uṣur,	Belshazzar
		uṣur		
l.25		māru	māru	the son
		reš		
		tu	reš-tu-ú	first (born)
		ú		
l.26		ṣi		
		it	ṣi-it	the offspring of
		lìb		
		bi	lìb-bi-ia	my heart (body)
		ia		

This reference is, of course, to Belshazzar who figures prominently in the Book of Daniel, where he is described as 'king' of Babylon (Dan. 5:1 etc.). It is clear from other inscriptions that Nabonidus spent several years of his reign in north-west Arabia during which Belshazzar ruled in Babylon in his place, and though he is not included in the king lists he was king in all but name during that time, and the Biblical statement may be understood in that light. The cuneiform texts show that the designation of Daniel as 'the third ruler in the kingdom' (Dan. 5:29) makes sense, Nabonidus (in Arabia) being first, and Belshazzar (in Babylon) being second. It is worth mentioning that the description of Nebuchadnezzar as the 'father' of Belshazzar in the Old Testament (Dan. 5:2, 11) is probably simply an example of the use of 'father' to mean forbear.

Cylinder inscription of
Nabonidus from Ur; 6th
century BC. Baked clay;
lth 10.4cm. WA 91125
(K 1689)

Babylonian Chronicle

This tablet forms part of a series which summarises the principal events of each year. Each annual entry is separated from the next by a horizontal line, and begins with a reference to the year of reign of the king in question. The present tablet, which covers the years 605 to 594 BC, is of particular interest from the point of view of Biblical Archaeology because of the entry for the seventh year of Nebuchadnezzar (598–7 BC). The text (lines 11–13 on the reverse) runs '11 In the seventh year, the month of Kislimu, the king of Akkad mustered his troops, marched to the Hatti-land, (l.12) and encamped against:

𒌷	ālu	the city of
𒅀	ia	
𒀀	a	ia-a-ḫu-du, 'Judah'
𒄷	ḫu	
𒁺	du	

and on the second day of the month of Addaru he seized the city and captured the king. (l.13) He appointed there a king of his heart, received its heavy tribute and sent (it) to Babylon'.

In this passage it is clear from the preceding entries that the 'king of Akkad' was Nebuchadnezzar, the 'Hatti-land' was Syria-Palestine, and the 'city of Judah' was Jerusalem. The text is therefore saying that Nebuchndnezzar led his army to Syria-Palestine, besieged Jerusalem and captured it.

The Babylonian year began in March-April of the western (Julian) calendar, and Kislimu, the ninth of the twelve months, which corresponded to November-December, fell in this instance in winter 598 BC. The 2nd of Addaru corresponded to 15th/16th (sunset to sunset) March of the western calendar so the importance of this text is that it fixes the date of the first fall of Jerusalem to 16 March 597 BC, an event referred to in 2 Kings 24:10–17, which identifies the deposed king as Jehoiakin (or Jehoiachin) and Nebuchadnezzar's nominee as Zedekiah.

The Babylonian month names Kislimu and Addaru correspond to the Hebrew *kislew*, Kislev (December/January; Zech. 7:1; Neh. 1:1) and *'adār*, 'Adar' (March/April; Ezra 6:15; Esth. 3.7 etc), because the Babylonian calendar appears to have been adopted in Palestine following the Babylonian conquest of the west in 605 BC. There are traces of an earlier, presumably Canaanite, calendar in the Old Testament, the four month names Abib (Deut. 16:1), Ziv (1 Ki. 6:1), Ethanim (1 Ki. 8:2) and Bul (1 Ki. 6:38) probably representing the equivalents of March/April, April/May, September/October and October/November of the western calendar respectively. This system had been superceded by one in which the months were referred to by number, and the Babylonian names are only found in such late books as Ezra, Nehemiah, Esther and Zechariah.

This document has a tantalising aspect because it ends with the year 594 BC, and the next surviving tablet in the series only takes up the story again in 556 BC, so the Babylonian evidence for the final destruction of Jerusalem, probably in 586 BC, is lacking.

On the basis of the script this tablet could have been inscribed at any time between 594 BC and the end of the Achaemenian period in 331 BC.

DOCUMENT 44   *Cyrus Cylinder*

This clay cylinder is inscribed in Babylonian cuneiform with an account by Cyrus, king of Persia 549–530 BC, of his conquest of Babylon in 539 BC and capture of Nabonidus, the last Babylonian king (see also Document 42). He claims to have achieved this with the aid of Marduk, the god of Babylon. He then describes measures of relief which he brought to the inhabitants of the city, and tells how he returned a number of god-images which Nabonidus had collected in Babylon, to their proper temples throughout Babylonia, Assyria and western Iran. At the same time he arranged for the restoration of these temples, and organised the return to their homelands of a number of people who had been held in Babylonia by the Babylonian kings. Though this account refers only to Mesopotamia and Iran it represents a policy which he carried out throughout his newly conquered empire, and the document transcribed in Ezra 6:3–5 authorising the rebuilding of the Jerusalem Temple, and the subsequent return of the Jews (Ezra 2) to Palestine, were manifestations of this policy.

This cylinder has sometimes been described as the 'first charter of human rights', but this reflects a misunderstanding. From as early as the third millennium BC kings in Mesopotamia often began their reigns with declarations of reforms, and this document simply follows in this long tradition.

Cyrus Cylinder from Babylon; 6th century BC. Baked clay; lth 23cm. WA 90920

Babylonian Chronicle for 605–594 BC from Babylon; 6th–4th century BC. Baked clay; ht (surviving) 8.1cm. WA 21946.

Trilingual Inscription of Darius I

This inscription, which is located high on a rock face on the main route from Ecbatana (modern Hamadan) to Babylonia, has been called the 'Rosetta Stone of cuneiform'. It bears an inscription of Darius I of Persia giving an account in Babylonian, Elamite and Old Persian of his suppression of a rebellion at the beginning of his reign. It provided the material for the decipherment of Old Persian and Babylonian as well as Elamite.

All three versions are inscribed in cuneiform but while the Babylonian script has over three hundred characters, and Elamite something over one hundred, the Old Persian script has only forty different signs (and a word-divider). Old Persian inscriptions had long been visible at Persepolis, the ceremonial capital of the Achaemenian kings, and several of these had been available in Europe in excellent copies since 1778 when these were published by the great Danish explorer Carsten Niebuhr, who had spent nearly a month at the site in 1765. On the basis of these copies George Grotefend was able to decipher the names Hystaspes, Darius and Xerxes, an acheivement he reported in a paper read in Göttingen in 1802. This formed the basis for further work by him and others, but in the absence of a substantial body of text not much progress followed. The major advance was made by Henry Creswick Rawlinson, an English officer of the Indian army who was stationed in Persia. His initial step arose from his observation, in 1835, that in the first columns of two trilingual inscriptions carved in the rock of Mount Elwend, the texts were identical with the exception of two short groups of signs in each, and that the first of these groups in one was the same as the second in the other. Guessing that these inscriptions might, like Pahlawi inscriptions known to him, give the names and titles of kings, he experimented with the idea that the sign groups in question were royal names. Assuming that the names in the two inscriptions represented A son of B, and B son of C, he tried the names of the first three Achaemenian kings, Hystaspes, Darius and Xerxes, in the forms known from Persian sources, and found that these worked. From this he learned the phonetic values of thirteen signs, thereby reaching much the same stage as that achieved by Grotefend over thirty years earlier, though the details of his work were unknown to Rawlinson at that time.

Rawlinson transferred his investigations to the Behistun inscription in 1836 and in that and the following year he succeeded in climbing up to and making a copy of the opening portion of the Old Persian text ('Persian' in the illustration). This portion records the titles and genealogy of Darius, and with his knowledge of Avestan (referred to at that time as Zend), he was able to complete a translation of this portion of the Old Persian text in 1837. Old Persian and Avestan are the main known dialects of Old Iranian, and Pahlawi is the best known of Middle Iranian. He returned to Behistun in 1844 and succeeded in copying the remainder of the Old Persian and the whole of the Elamite ('Susian' in the illustration) versions, and published a translation of the complete Old Persian text in 1847. In the preparation of this he was much helped by a commentary on the Yasna, part of the Avesta, published in 1833 by Eugène Burnouf.

The Babylonian text is located on a projecting rock higher up than the rest, and Rawlinson only succeeded in copying this in 1847 with the help of an agile Kurdish boy who took a paper impression ('squeeze') of it. This version could be seen to use a much more complicated script, but by matching the proper names (conveniently signalled by preceding determinative signs) with those already deciphered in the Old Persian version, Rawlinson was able to obtain the values of a number of signs; for example 'Darius' was written *da-a-ra-ya-va-u-ša* in Old Persian and *da-ri-ia-muš* in Babylonian. Applying the phonetic values determined in this way, Rawlinson and others found that the language of the text as a whole could be illuminated by parallels from

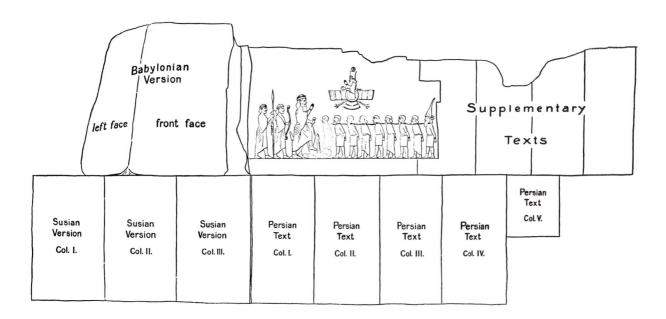

Trilingual inscription of Darius I (521–485 BC) carved on the rock at Behistun, Iran; 5th century BC. Ht of Babylonian version 7.78cm

Semitic languages such as Hebrew, Syriac and Arabic. When Old Persian *a-da-ma* (Avestan *azem*), 'I', was found, for instance, to be rendered in Babylonian by *a-na-ku*, the similarity with Hebrew *'ānōkî*, 'I', was clear. Subsequent study showed that Babylonian was indeed a Semitic language (see above). The decipherment of Babylonian gave the key to an immense body of inscribed material from Mesopotamia, and the large number of inscribed clay tablets already in Museums at the time of the decipherment has been greatly increased since by excavation (see above).

Cylinder Seal of Parshandata

Seals of this kind, which were rolled across clay tablets or sealings to leave their impressions, were used in the ancient Near East from the third millennium until Achaemenian times, after which they were largely replaced by stamp seals (see Documents 34, 35, 39). This example, of chalcedony, which is decorated with a scene of the king confronting two mythical beasts below the winged symbol of Ahura-Mazda, is typical of the Achaemenian period. It is of particular interest because of the inscription in the Aramaic alphabet which reads:

ʮ ʌ ʮ	ḥtm	seal of
ʌ ʮ ⱴ ʮ]	pršndt	Parshandata
ʮ ʯ	br	son of
ʝ ʌ ʮ ʮ ⱴ ✶	ʾrtdtn	ʾArtadatan

The word for 'seal' does not occur in the Aramaic portions of the Old Testament, but the Hebrew cognate *hōtām* is found for instance in the very familiar account of how Jezebel obtained Naboth's vineyard for her husband Ahab by forging letters in his name and sealing them with his seal in order to secure the murder of Naboth (1 Kings 21:8).

The name Parshandata finds an exact consonantal correspondence in the name of one of the Persian inhabitants of Susa mentioned in the book of Esther (Est. 9:7) where his name is spelled *paršandātāʾ*, Parshandatha in the Authorised Version.

Cylinder seal of
Parshandata, Achaemenian;
5th century BC.
Chalcedony; ht 3.5cm.
WA 89152

Rosetta Stone

This inscribed stone slab was discovered in 1799 by Lieutenant P.F.X. Bouchard, a French officer of Napoleon's army, in the western Delta of Egypt, and was surrendered to the British according to the Treaty of Capitulation which ended the war. It came to the British Museum in 1802. The stone, a black basalt, partially broken away, bears the remains of a bilingual, Egyptian-Greek, inscription in three scripts. The Egyptian text is given in both the hieroglyphic (14 lines surviving), and demotic (32 lines) scripts, and the Greek version (51 lines) is in Greek uncial (capital) letters.

The Greek text was soon translated, the Reverend S. Weston reading a paper on it before the Society of Antiquaries in 1802. It contains a decree issued by the assembly of Egyptian priests in Memphis to celebrate the first anniversary of the coronation of Ptolemy V Epiphanes, 204–180 BC, which had taken place in his eighth year, 197 BC, the inscription therefore dating from 196 BC.

The Rosetta stone played a major, though not exclusive, part in the decipherment of the Egyptian hieroglyphics, the clue coming from comparison of the writing of

Rosetta Stone from near Rashid (Rosetta), Delta, Egypt; 196 BC. Ht 115cm.
E 24

proper names. The positions and frequency of these were clear from the Greek text. Already in 1802 the French scholar Silvestre de Sacy and the Swedish diplomat J.D. Åkerblad had identified all the names appearing in the Demotic version, together with a few other words. These results came into the hands of the English polymath Thomas Young (1773–1829). Unlike de Sacy and Åkerblad he recognised that the hieroglyphic and demotic scripts were closely related and that these scripts made use of signs not only with single (alphabetic) sound values but also syllabic and word values. He worked at the demotic version first, identifying the most frequently written, and therefore most easily recognisable, sign groups, ''Ptolemy'' 'Egypt', 'king' and 'and'. He then turned his attention to the hieroglyphic version in which he adopted the suggestion, already made by others, that groups of signs enclosed in oval lines (cartouches) gave the names of rulers. The only royal name in the surviving hieroglyphic text on the Rosetta Stone is Ptolemy, spelled *ptolemaios* in the Greek, and since the cartouche contains seven characters the values *p-t-o-l-m-i-s* (now transliterated *p-t-w'r-m-y-s*) could be proposed. He was then able to identify the name 'Berenike', whose cartouche he found next to that of her husband Ptolemy I Soter, on a different monument. These names had two characters in common, *i(y)* and *t* (in an unpronounced feminine ending in *brnyk't*), supporting his suppositions.

Further advances were made by the Englishman W.J. Bankes with the aid of the hieroglyphic text on a granite obelisk from Philae, which he brought back to his home at Kingston Lacey in Dorset. A stone plinth found near it and probably belonging to it bears three related Greek inscriptions giving the names of Ptolemy (IX Euergetes II) and of his queen, Cleopatra. These names correspond to two cartouches in the hieroglphic text in which Bankes found that they had two characters in common, *p* and *l(r)*. Further, when he noted that a presumed third consonant, *t*, was represented by two different characters he was able to conclude that homophony ('same sound') of different hieroglyphs was a characteristic of the Egyptian script.

The identification of the hieroglyphs used to write the names Ptolemy, Berenike and Cleopatra, set the process of decipherment on course. It was carried on beyond the simple matching up of proper names by the French scholar Jean François Champollion (1790–1832), who, with the aid of Coptic (late Egyptian written in an adapted form of the Greek alphabet), was able to publish an account of the essentials of the decipherment in 1822, and a fuller description of the Egyptian writing system in 1824, which formed the basis of all future work and made possible the translation of Egyptian literature.

The hieroglyphic script would have been familiar to the Hebrews during their time in Egypt and it may be assumed that Moses, who is said to have been adopted by Pharaoh's daughter (Ex. 2:10), would have learned to read and probably write it. This is not stated in the Old Testament, but in the speech given by Stephen reported in the book of Acts, Moses is described as having been 'instructed in all the wisdom of the Egyptians' (7:22). This could well reflect a specific tradition not recorded in the Old Testament.

Letter from Isias to Hephaestion

Letter from Isaias to
Hephaestion from
Memphis, Egypt; 168 BC.
Papyrus; lth 32.1cm.
BL Papyrus 42

This Papyrus letter is from an Egyptian woman named Isias to her husband Hephaestion, who was in temporary religious seclusion in the Serapeum at Memphis. She tells him of the difficulties she had experienced in supporting herself and his child during his absence, and says that she heard that his period of seclusion was finished and had hoped that she would get some relief on his return. She also adds that his mother is worried about him, and begs him to come home.

While the letter is earlier in date than the New Testament, having been written in the time of Ptolemy VI Philomotor, of Egypt 180–145 BC, when Palestine was under the rule of Antiochus IV, Epiphanes, 175–164 BC, it is written in the ordinary colloquial Greek, or *Koine*, which is the language of much of the New Testament. The *koinē*, or 'common', Greek, had developed from the Attic dialect which had begun to be used in trade and diplomacy beyond the area of immediate Athenian control already in the fifth and fourth centuries BC. With the conquests of Alexander the Great, in the late fourth century, language followed political domination, and Greek became the *lingua franca* of the ancient world in the Hellenistic period.

Greek papyri discovered in Egypt have helped to illuminate the grammar and vocabulary of the New Testament. The present example does not offer any spectacular demonstration of this, but an instance is the word used to express the 'relief' Isias hoped to find when her husband should return home [line 19]. The word *anapsuchis*, meaning 'cooling', 'refreshing', 'relief', occurs in the later spelling *anapsuxis* in the New Testament in Acts 3:19 (Greek 3:20), where Peter is reported as calling for repentance so that that sins of his hearers may be blotted out and times of spiritual refreshment (*anapsuxeos*) may come from the presence of the Lord. The verb from which *anapsuchis* derives, namely *anapsuchō*, 'to cool' (basically 'to cool with a breath'), is used in Paul's Second Letter to Timothy 1:16 where he calls for God's mercy on Onesiphorus because he had often 'refreshed' (*anepsuxen*) him, Paul, when he was in custody in Rome.

A more general point of some significance illustrated by this letter, and many others like it, is that the New Testament 'epistles' follow the general form or pattern of letters of the time. The present example begins *isias hephaistiōni tōi adelpho[i chai(rein)]*, 'Isias to Hephaistion her brother[r (i.e. husband) greeting]', the latter part being damaged but restored on the basis of many other examples. An abbreviation of *chairein*, 'greeting', is assumed on grounds of space. This pattern is found in the letter concerning Paul quoted in Acts 23:26–30, which begins *klaudios lusias tōi kratistōi hegemoni pheliki chairein*, 'Claudius Lysias to the most excellent governor Felix greeting' (cf. also Acts 15:23). Among the New Testament epistles that of James begins (1:1), *iakōbos....tais dodeka phulais...chairein*, 'James...to the twelve tribes...greeting', the recipient being, of course, a group rather than an individual.

The letters of Paul, though they have much more elaborate openings, follow the same general pattern. The two Letters to Timothy, for instance, begin *paulos...timotheōi...charis, eleos, eirēnē apo theou patros kai christou iēsou tou kuriou hēmōn*, 'Paul...to Timothy...grace, mercy, peace from God the Father and Christ Jesus our Lord' (1 Tim. 1:1-2; 2 Tim. 1:1-2), and the letter to Titus begins in virtually the same way (1:1-4). The formulae opening the letters to churches also follow the same pattern, as, for instance, Romans *paulos...pasin tois ousin en rhōmē...charis humin kai eirēnē apo theou patros hēmōn kai kuriou iesou christou*, 'Paul...to all that are in Rome...grace to you and peace from God our Father and the Lord Jesus Christ' (Rom. 1:1-7).

The often lengthy concluding messages and greetings in the Pauline letters are also partially paralleled by the present example which, in spite of its chiding tone, concludes 'Pray take care of yourself that you may be in health'.

Scroll jar

Scroll jar from Qumran, 1st century AD. Ht 56cm. WA 131444

One of the most notable archaeological discoveries of the twentieth century was that in 1947 of a number of Hebrew manuscripts, dating from the New Testament era, in caves in cliffs near the northwest shore of the Dead Sea. These were found to have been deposited in the caves for safekeeping by the members of a religious community which had occupied a complex of buildings, known as Khirbet Qumran, near the foot of the cliffs. The manuscripts, which are mainly in Hebrew, include sectarian documents of the community as well as parts of the Old Testament which provide evidence of the form of the text before the time of the Massoretes and in fact nearly a thousand years earlier than the greater number of the Old Testament manuscripts known up to the time of the discovery (see Document 60).

The sectarian documents contribute to a view of the background of New Testament times by preserving a record of some of the beliefs and practices of a particular religious sect, probably the Essenes.

The Biblical manuscripts have opened up a new period in the study of the text of the Old Testament. It has long been known that among the many surviving Greek manuscripts of the New Testament there exist a number of variant readings, and that it was a reasonable thing to study these with a view to arriving at the Greek text as near as possible to that originally written (see Document 59). A quite different situation was thought to exist for the Old Testament because the surviving manuscripts represented texts which differed very little from each other. It was known that in the early centuries of the Christian era Jewish scholars had worked to standardise the Hebrew text, and this work culminated in the tenth century with the closely related texts prepared by scholars of the Ben Asher family and by Ben Naphtali.

The manuscripts of the Old Testament from Qumran, where every book except Esther is represented, preserve some texts which differ from the long familiar Massoretic version. Some reflect a Hebrew text nearer to that probably lying behind that found in the Greek translation known as the Septuagint (see Document 59) and others appear to come closer to the Samaritan Pentateuch. The significance of these observations is that it can be recognised that the same situation obtained with regard to the Old Testament text as that long known of the New, namely that copying and recopying of the original manuscripts had led to variants, and scholars must take this into account and study to determine the form of text nearest to that originally written.

Head of Augustus Caesar

Gaius Octavius, the first Roman Emperor, great nephew and subsequently adopted son of Julius Caesar, became supreme ruler in 29 BC, and received the name *Augustus*, 'worthy of honour', from the Senate in 27 BC. He was the emperor in power at the time of the birth of Jesus, as is stated in Luke 2:1, where he is referred to as Caesar Augustus, the Latin name Augustus being transliterated into Greek as *augustos*. The name Augustus was subsequently taken by most of the following emperors.

Bronze head of Augustus
Caesar 27 BC–AD14 from
Meroe, Sudan. Ht 43cm.
GR 1911.9–1.1

Bust of Tiberius Caesar

Tiberius Claudius Nero was the stepson and subsequently son-in-law of Augustus (Document 50) and was adopted as his heir following the deaths of Augustus' adopted grandsons Gaius and Lucius Caesar. When Augustus died, the Senate conferred the full imperial powers on Tiberius. He was Emperor during the years of Jesus's ministry and at the time of his crucifixion. He is referred to as Tiberius Caesar, in Luke 3:1, and simply as Caesar elsewhere in the Gospels (Matt 22:17,21; Mark 12: 14, 16, 17; Luke 20:22, 24, 25; 23:2; John 19:12, 15).

Bust of Tiberius Caesar
AD14–37 from the Burke
Collection. Ht 48cm.
GR 1812.6–15.5

Head of Claudius Caesar

Tiberius Claudius Caesar, generally known as Claudius, was proclaimed Emperor by the Praetorian Guard after the murder of Gaius, generally known as 'Caligula' (AD.37-41), who does not appear in the Bible. Claudius was Emperor when the early Church was growing, and he is mentioned in the book of Acts as the ruler in whose time a famine took place (Acts 11:28). When the Jews of Thessalonica accused Paul and Silas of violating Caesar's decrees by claiming that Jesus is the king, he was the Emperor in question (Acts 17:7), and he is mentioned by name as having expelled the Jews from Rome, Aquila and Priscilla being among those who came east at that time (Acts 18:2).

Head of Claudius Caesar AD41–54 from the Temple of Athena Polias at Priene, Asia Minor, presented by the Society of Dilettanti. Ht 47.6cm. GR 1870.3–20.200

Head of Nero

Nero Claudius Caesar, generally known as Nero, was the last ruler in the Julio–Claudian dynasty founded by Augustus. He was Emperor in the time of Paul and is the 'Caesar' to whom he appealed for justice (Acts 25:21; 28:19). He is referred to in Acts 25:21 and 25 by the title *sebastos*, the Greek translation of Latin *augustus*, rendered 'Emperor' in the English versions, a title first conferred on Augustus (see Document 50), and used by most of his successors.

Head of Nero AD54–68 brought from Athens to England by Anthony Askew in 1740 and acquired by Charles Townley before 1776. Ht 43cm. GR 1805.7–3.246

Papyrus Census Order

Papyrus Census Order
from Egypt; AD 104. Ht
22.2cm. BL Papyrus 904

A papyrus document containing a command in Greek from the Prefect Gaius Vibius
Maximus for all those in his area of authority to return to their own homes for the
purposes of a census (*apographēs*). This illustrates a situation in the time of Trajan
analogous to that described by Luke at the time of the birth of Christ (Lk. 2:1–4),
when Augustus (see Document 50) decreed that a census (*apographēs*) should be taken
of the Roman world.

Fragments of an Unknown Gospel

Two papyrus pages inscribed on both sides in ink in Greek with the text of four passages concerning Jesus. These fragments, and a third containing only a few words, were acquired from a dealer in 1934, but may be presumed to have been discovered in Egypt. The palaeography of the script suggests a date around 150 AD, making these fragments only about twenty years later than the earliest known Gospel manuscript, a papyrus fragment in the John Rylands Library in Manchester, dated palaeographically to about 130 AD, which preserves a small portion of John's Gospel (18:31–33, 37–38).

These fragments come from a codex, that is to say a book bound like a modern one with pages in quires, rather than a rolled up scroll. The four sides contain seventy-five lines of text which give extracts narrating: I, an encounter between Jesus and some lawyers (lines 1–31); II, the healing of a leper by Jesus (32–41); III, an encounter between Jesus and some critics (43–59); and IV, a miracle performed by Jesus in which he apparently sows seed on the River Jordan and it immediately bears fruit (60–75). Extract I has affinities with a number of passages in the first three (the Synoptic) Gospels (Matt. 8:2–4; Mk. 1:40–44; Lk. 5:12–14) and III reflects passages in all four Gospels (Matt. 15:7–8; 22:15–18; Mk. 7:6–7; 12:13–15; Lk. 6:46; 20:20–23; Jn. 3:2; 10:25). Though these three extracts thus reflect many passages in the known Gospels, they do not represent parallel quotations from them. It appears probable that they were written by an author who knew the four canonical Gospels, and possibly had them before him as he wrote, and that he paraphrased them in order to provide a work of instruction.

These documents, by thus evidently quoting from the canonical Gospels, serve as evidence of their existence by the middle of the second century AD. By Canonical is meant those books belonging to the canon of Scripture, the list of books recognised by the church as authoritative. The dates of composition of the canonical Gospels are debated but one moderate view would place Mark around AD 65, Luke shortly before AD 70, Matthew shortly after this, and John not long before AD 100, dates consistent with the evidence of these fragments.

The second extract (II) begins with the leper addressing Jesus with the words *didaskale iē(sou)*, 'Master Jesus', a combination not found in the New Testament. The abbreviated spelling of the name of Jesus IH, *iē*, may be seen in the twelfth surviving line of the second side of the first fragment. This is a shorter form of the abbreviation IHS, the first three letters of the names *iēsous*, which is so often seen in modern church decoration. (For H as the Greek long *ē*, see Document 6.)

The fourth extract (IV) is of a different kind from the first three. The miracle described, which is quite unknown in the canonical Gospels, has a flavour of magic and shows that the composition falls into the category known as New Testament Apocrypha. The well known Apocrypha which is often found bound with the English Bible, comprises some of the Jewish books which did not form part of the Old Testament canon. A considerable number of compositions have survived in the form of Gospels, Acts, Epistles and Apocalypses, which bear the same sort of relation to the New Testament canon and are known as New Testament Apocrypha. They often show signs of being imaginative inventions, perhaps composed by devout Christians, seeking mistakenly to honour Jesus Christ. This type of material has little historical value.

Fragments of an unknown
Gospel probably from
Egypt; *c.* 150AD. Lths 11.5,
11.8 and 6cm. BL Papyrus
Egerton 2

Politarch Inscription

A Greek inscription from a Roman gateway at Thessalonica (modern Salonika) in northern Greece (ancient Macedonia). The inscription lists the officials of the town in the second century AD, beginning with six Politarchs and naming the city Treasurer and the Gymnasiarch (Director of Higher Education). The inscription begins *poleitarchounton*, 'While [the following] were acting as Politarchs', from the verb *politarcheō*, 'to act as Politarch'. This verb and the noun *politarchēs* with which it is cognate are known from a number of inscriptions and refer to the magistrates of cities. The largest group come from Macedonia, five of them from Thessalonica, showing that the city had five Politarchai in the early first century AD and six in the second century.

According to the Book of Acts, Paul and Silas, while in Thessalonica, gathered a number of converts; certain Jews incited the city to an uproar and Christians were accused before the *politarchas*, 'rulers of the city' (AV, RV) 'city authorities' (RSV) of being trouble-makers (Acts 17:6, 8). They were subsequently allowed to go, and Paul and Silas travelled on during the night to Beroea.

It is worth noting that two of the names that appear in this inscription, Sosipatros (*sōsipatrou*, line 1) and Lucius (*loukiou*, line 1) were borne by two men at Beroea whom Paul describes as *sungenēs*, literally 'kinsmen', but in this context perhaps Jewish Christians (Romans 16:21). Equally, the names Secundus (*sekoundo[u]*, line 2) and Gaius (*gaiou*, line 5) were born by a man from Thessalonica (Acts 20:4), and a Macedonian (Acts 19:29), who were travelling companions of Paul. These were not, of course, the same men, but simply demonstrate the currency of the personal names in the area in the century following the time of Paul.

Politarch Inscription from Thessalonica; 2nd century AD, presented by J E Blunt in 1877. Limestone; ht 82.5cm. GR 1877.5–11.1

DOCUMENT 57 — *Coin from Ephesus*

A bronze coin of the time of the Roman Emperor Antoninus Pius AD 138–161, minted in Ephesus. The obverse shows the head of the Emperor and the reverse the Temple of Artemis, the principal goddess of the city. The columns supporting the pediment are shown with sculptured bases, one example of which is exhibited in the Department of Greek and Roman Antiquities (BM Sculp. 1206). Between the columns, representing the inside of the temple, is depicted the image of the goddess, which the Ephesians believed had fallen from heaven (Acts 19:35). Paul, who spent some time at Ephesus, as described in Acts 19, fell foul of the silversmiths because they thought he was undermining their trade of selling silver shrines of the goddess. The Authorised and Revised Versions of the Bible give the name of the goddess in this passage as Diana (Acts 19:24, 27–28, 34–35), but this is simply a substitution of the Roman or Latin name for the Greek form Artemis, which is what appears in the Greek text, and this is the rendering of the New English Bible.

The Greek inscription on the obverse of the coin reads *ephesiōn*, 'of [the] Ephesians', and *dis neōkorōn*, 'twice temple keeper' being a title granted to several cities in Asia Minor which built and maintained temples in honour of the Roman emperor. The 'twice' indicates that Ephesus was 'temple keeper' also of the Temple of Artemis, a fact referred to in the speech of the town clerk (*grammateus*) of Ephesus, quoted in Acts, who, having quietened the mob who were against Paul, tried to placate them by saying that everyone knew that 'the city of the Ephesians is temple-keeper (*neōkoron*) of the great Artemis' (Acts 19:35).

Bronze coin from Ephesus; 2nd century AD. Diam 3.77cm, wt 17.33gm. BMC Ephesus 234

DOCUMENT 58 — *Bronze Assarion*

Bronze coin minted on Chios, a small island off the west coast of Asia Minor. The obverse shows a seated sphinx with the inscription *chiōn*, 'of [the] Chians', and the reverse an amphora and the inscription *assarion*. The word *assarion* is a Hellenised form of the Latin denomination *as* which, beginning at a weight of over 255 grammes in the third century BC in Roman Republican times, had been reduced in value by the first and second centuries AD to something near to ten grammes. The denomination was widely used in the Aegean and Asia Minor, usually with a still lighter weight.

A coin named the *assariōn* rendered 'farthing' in the AV and RV, and 'penny' in the NEB, figures in an encouraging statement by Jesus to his disciples (Matt. 10:29 and Lk. 12:6), the point of which is that if God takes care even of sparrows, how much more will he care for them. In Matthew the value of sparrows is given as two for one *assarion*, while in Luke the value is five for two *assaria*. This minor discrepancy could stem from slightly different recollections of the saying, the sense being unaffected.

Bronze Assarion from Chios; 2nd century AD. Diam 1.9cm, wt 4.99gm. BMC Chios 127

This manuscript, bound in codex form, like a modern book, is inscribed in Greek uncial (capital) letters, in ink on parchment (treated leather). It originally contained the whole Old and New Testaments as well as the Old Testament Apocryphal books Tobit, Judith, 1 to 4 Maccabees, Wisdom and Ecclesiasticus, and, with the New Testament, two books (the Epistle of Barnabas and the Shepherd of Hermas) belonging to the category generally known as the Apostolic Fathers. Though about 300 pages are missing from the manuscript, these belong to the Old Testament section while the New Testament is complete.

The manuscript was discovered by the German scholar Constantine Tischendorf at the Eastern Orthodox Monastery of St. Catharine in the Sinai Penisula in 1844, when he saw some pages among others waiting to be burned as rubbish. He was able to rescue them and was allowed to take away forty-three sheets which he presented to Frederick Augustus of Saxony, and this portion, known as the Codex Frederico-Augustanus, is still in the Court Library at Leipzig. Tischendorf obtained the remainder

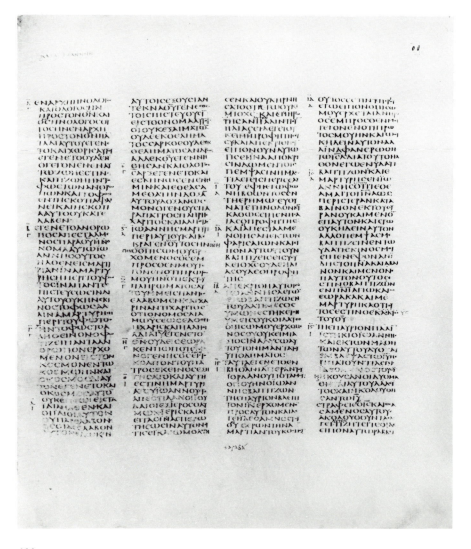

Codex Sinaiticus from St Catherine's Monastery, Sinai; 4th century AD, showing the beginning of the Gospel of John. Ht 38cm. BL Add. MS. 43725

of the surviving part of the manuscript in 1859 and presented it to the Russian Tsar, a senior figure in the Eastern Orthodox Church, a somewhat irregular transaction which was regularised in 1869. It was purchased from the Russian authorities by the British Museum in 1933.

While the Codex Sinaiticus provides a witness, albeit seriously marred by the absence of substantial sections, to the Greek text of the Old Testament known as the Septuagint, the New Testament portion, which was complete, made the most impact in the world of Biblical scholarship.

Since the time of the Reformation the Greek New Testament prepared by Desiderius Erasmus and first published in 1516 held a preeminent position, and indeed came to be known as the 'Textus Receptus' or 'Received Text' on the basis of a claim made by the Leiden publishing house of Elzevir in their edition published in 1633, that the reader now had the text received by all. Ignorance of the insubstantial origin of this designation led to a strong resistance to any modification of this text. Erasmus had, however, derived it from a very limited number of Greek manuscripts dating only from the twelfth and thirteenth centuries AD. Though the unsatisfactory nature of this text made no serious difference to the broad sweep of the New Testament message, and the Authorised Version served many generations very well, the discovery of earlier manuscripts made it increasingly clear to a small number of scholars that a better Greek text was a possibility. Tischendorf himself helped to further the practical achievement of this when he published an edition of the Greek text in 1869–72 in which he recorded variant readings from sixty-four uncial texts (including Sinaiticus), one papyrus, and a small number of other texts. This took him many years to prepare, and he was not able to make use of the readings of another great uncial manuscript, the Codex Vaticanus, in the Vatican Library in Rome (an edition of which was published in 1857). Two nineteenth century English scholars B.F. Westcott and F.J.A. Hort, however, saw in it a superior text to that preserved in Sinaiticus, and made extensive use of it in their Greek New Testament which was published in 1881, and which formed the basis of the Revised Version of the New Testament, published in the same year.

It was thus widely accepted by the end of the nineteenth century that among the manuscripts of the New Testament there existed many variant readings, the result of scribal errors in transmission, and that it was reasonable to study these intensively to try to arrive at a text as near as possible to that originally written. There are today well over 3000 manuscripts of parts or all of the New Testament, and the discipline of Textual Criticism has produced resulting texts of increasing quality.

The same situation of variant manuscripts of the Old Testament has become clear in the forty years since the manuscript find at Qumran by the Dead Sea (see Document 49).

Hebrew Pentateuch

This manuscript of the Hebrew Pentateuch is in codex form (like a modern bound book and not a scroll) in which the opening and closing pages are vulnerable to loss by damage. In this instance the first 39 chapters of Genesis and all but the first chapter of Deuteronomy are missing, as well as two short passages in Numbers. The surviving portion, however, represents a good example of the type of medieval manuscript in which the Hebrew text used by all students of the Old Testament until the discovery of the Dead Sea Scrolls (see Document 49) was preserved.

The text is written in an elegant clear script, with the vowel 'points' according to the system developed at Tiberias in Palestine, the culmination of about five centuries (fifth to tenth) of experiment in the representation of the vowels.

The script is virtually that generally known as the 'Square Script' familiar in printed form in modern Hebrew Bibles. Though (apart from distinguishing between š and ś by means of a supralinear dot) the number and values of the characters are the same as those of the archaic or Old Hebrew script, the forms are clearly quite different (see Document 6). This is because the Jews, who had used the Old Hebrew script throughout the period of the Monarchy, found a different form of the alphabetic script in use alongside cuneiform in Babylonia when they arrived there is Exile in the sixth century BC. This script had developed from the Aramaic branch of the alphabet which, language and script together, was widely used in Assyria and Babylonia from the eighth century BC onwards. The Jews adopted this script during the course of the Exile and it developed in time into the familiar Square Script. The Old Hebrew script was thereafter used only for special purposes, such as for writing the name *yhwh*, 'Yahweh', in religious texts otherwise in the Aramaic script, and in a nationalistic spirit on coins of the Maccabaean period.

The page shown in the illustration, which runs from the middle of Exodus 19:24 to the middle of 20:17, includes most of the ten commandments. The text runs from right to left, and the spaced-out passage at the bottom of the left hand column gives the short commandments of the decalogue. The three short lines run

tirṣāḥ lō'	(v.13) you shall kill. (v.14) Not
tin'ap lō'	you shall commit adultery. (v.15) Not
tignōb lō'	you shall steal. (v.16) Not

These commandments would normally be written *lō' tirṣāḥ*, *lō' tin'āp* and *lō' tignōb*, the *lō'*, ('not') belonging to *tirṣāḥ*, in this case appearing in the line above.

Hebrew Pentateuch, provenance unknown; 9th century AD. Ht 42cm. BL Or. 4445

מרחק ח חסילוז ויעמד על ראש ההר יהוה אלהי אתה ארוממך יתשלחי עיניך דאר ורב אני נאט יהוה אהבי וריעי מנגר
יבא אוריתא רכומהו ׃ וידבר אלהים ׃ ויסימנהה נח משה הדבריס סינח ב בה ד יונה בכל גו ביוט השביעי ס

לך דד ועל תאתעד
ואהרן ועמך וחכהעם
וחעאס אל יהרסו
לעלת אל יהוה פן
יפרץ בם סור משה
אל הדעס ויאמר
אלהם ׃ וידבר
אלהים את כל
הדברים ׃ האלה
לאמר ׀ אנכי
יהוה אלהיך אשר
הוצאתיך מארץ
מצרים מבית עבדיס
לא יהיה לך אלהים
אחרים על פני לא
תעשה לך פסל
וכל תמונה אשר
בשמים ממעל ואשר
בארץ מתחת ואשר
במים מתחת לארץ
לא תשתחוה להם

ולא תעבדם ׀ כי
אנכי יהוה אלהיך
אל קנא פקד עון
אבת על בנים על
שלשים ורבעים
לשנאי ועשה חסד
לאלפים לאהבי
ולשמרי מצותי
לא תשא את
שס יהוה אלהיך
לשוא כי לא ינקה
יהוה את אשר ישא
את שמו לשוא ׃
זמור את יום השבת
לקדשו ששת ימים
תעבד ועשית כל
מלאכתך ויום
השביעי שבת
ליהוה אלהיך לא
תעשה כל מלאכה

אתה ובנך ובתך
עבדך ואמתך
ובהמתך וגרך אשר
בשעריך כי ששת
ימים עשה יהוה
את השמים ואת
הארץ את היס ואת
כל אשר בס וינח
ביום השביעי על
כן ברך יהוה את יום
השבת ויקדשהו ׃
כבד את אביך
ואת אמך למען
יארכון ימיך על
האדמה אשר יהוה
אלהיך נתן לך לא
תרצח ׃ לא
תנאף ׃ לא
תגנב ׃ לא
תענה ברעך עד שקר
לא תחמד בית

ג פסוק וחנז מן תרירתו תריכזו קדמא ז וכיומנזה ש וסרימנזה הׁ השבצ שמור אכ זום חשבצ ואולפלת שם העיר
ואולפ לזש שם לא תזבח לא תשחמט ס וחלופיאזן ג יוטבין חזרמא ז שלה יהוזדע יתנזרע למו שבזחמת ו
למה זנחתנו אשזמלדה אמרי ה סח פסזק איתבהון לא לא לא לא תרזבצ רולה שמות וחפזה לא כפרתח ומלזתיך בניס
חזרזט לא אבל אדיוס לא עממזו הנבחדזוזל לא יפקד לא שמזעה בקזול ס

Further Reading

Abbreviations

ANEP: J.B. Pritchard (ed.), *The Ancient Near East in Pictures Relating to the Old Testament* (3rd ed.; Princeton, 1970).

ANET: J.B. Pritchard (ed.), *Ancient Near Eastern Texts Relating to the Old Testament* (3rd ed.; Princeton, 1969).

BASOR: *Bulletin of the American Schools of Oriental Research* (New Haven).

BMOP: *British Museum Occasional Papers.*

CAD: *Chicago Assyrian Dictionary.*

CAH: I.E.S. Edwards et al. (eds.), *The Cambridge Ancient History* (Cambridge), I.1 (1970), 2 (1971), II.1 (1973), 2 (1975), III.1 (1982), 2 (in preparation), 3 (1982) and continuing.

CII: *Corpus Inscriptionum Iranicarum* (London).

CIS: *Corpus Inscriptionum Semiticarum* (Paris).

CIWA: H.C. Rawlinson et al., *Cuneiform Inscriptions of Western Asia*, I (London, 1861), II (1866), III (1870), IV (1875; 2nd ed.; 1891), V (1880–84). Referred to in the literature as IR, IIR etc.

DOTT: D.W. Thomas (ed.), *Documents from Old Testament Times* (Edinburgh, 1958; repr., New York, 1965).

IOTH: R.D. Barnett, *Illustrations of Old Testament History* (2nd ed.; British Museum; London, 1976).

JRAS: *Journal of the Royal Asiatic Society* (London).

KAI: H. Donner and W. Röllig, *Kanaanäische und Aramäische Inschriften* (Wiesbaden, 1962–64).

NERTROT: W. Beyerlin (ed.), *Near Eastern Religious Texts Relating to the Old Testament* (London, 1978).

PSBA: *Proceedings of the Society of Biblical Archaeology* (London).

TGI: K. Galling (ed.), *Textbuch zur Geschichte Israels* (2nd ed,; Tubingen, 1968).

TSBA: *Transactions of the Society of Biblical Archaeology* (London).

TSSI: J.C.L. Gibson, *Textbook of Syrian Semitic Inscriptions* (Oxford), I *Hebrew and Moabite Inscriptions* (1971), II *Aramaic Inscriptions* (1975), III *Phoenician Inscriptions* (1982).

TUAT: O. Kaiser (ed.), *Texte aus der Umwelt des Alten Testaments* (Gütersloh, 1982).

ZA: *Zeitschrift für Assyriologie* (Berlin).

Notes to Introduction and the Documents

A number in brackets following a shortened book title indicates that the full reference is given in the note on the Document bearing that number. Other shortened titles are given in full above.

p.7. Works confined to Palestine: eg. K.M. Kenyon (rev. by P.R.S. Moorey) *The Bible and Recent Archaeology* (London, 1987); G.E. Wright, *Biblical Archaeology* (2nd ed.; London, 1962). Society of Biblical Archaeology: aims set out in TSBA I (1872) pp. i–iv; see also in general E.A.W. Budge, *The Rise and Progress of Assyriology* (London, 1925), pp. 261–5.

Rembrandt etching: A.M. Hind, *A Catalogue of Rembrandt's Etchings* (rev. ed.; British Museum; London, 1923), I, no. 149, II, pl. 149.

p.8. Danish expedition: T. Hansen, *Arabia Felix. The Danish Expedition of 1761-67* (New York, 1964).

p.9. Early Biblical criticism: see in general S. Terrien in G.A. Buttrick et al. (eds.), *The Interpreters Bible* I (New York, 1952), pp. 130–132, and bibliography p. 141.

Early excavations in Mesopotamia: see Seton Lloyd, *Foundations in the Dust* (rev. ed.; London, 1980) pp. 1–129; and in Egypt W.R. Dawson and E.P. Uphill, *Who Was Who In Egyptology* (2nd ed.; London 1972) under the relevant names.

Birch's inaugural address: PSBA 1 (1872), pp. 1–12.

Early excavations in Palestine: W.F. Albright, *The Archaeology of Palestine* (4th ed.; London, 1960), pp. 26–34; Silberman, *Digging* (no. 18).

p.10. Driver quotation: *Modern Research as Illustrating the Bible* [Schweich

Lectures, 1908] (London, 1922), p. 87; on late Bronze Age destruction levels in Palestine and the related problems: eg. J.M. Miller in J.H. Hayes and J.M. Miller, *Israelite and Judaean History* (London, 1977), pp. 252–62. Palestinian pottery: R. Amiran, *The Pottery of the Holy Land* (Jerusalem, 1963).

Results of excavations: see M. Avi Yonah (ed.), *Encyclopedia of Archaeological Excavations in the Holy Land*, I–IV (London, 1975–8).

Smith quotation: G. Smith, *Assyrian Discoveries. An Account of Explorations and Discoveries on the Site of Nineveh During 1873 and 1874* (London, 1875), p. 9.

p.11. Scripts: hieroglyphic, see Davies, *Hieroglyphs* (no. 47); cuneiform, see Walker, *Cuneiform* (no. 45); alphabetic, see bibliography under no. 6.

p.12. 'Yahua son of Hubiri': Rawlinson, JRAS 12 (1850), p. 447; read as 'Jehu, son of Omri' by E. Hinks, *Athenaeum* (1851), p. 1384; see also E.F. Davidson, *Edward Hincks. A Selection from his Correspondence with A. Memoir* (Oxford, 1933), pp. 167, 171, 193, 194.

pp.15–17. The dates for the Monarchy are those of E.R. Thiele in *The Mysterious Numbers of the Hebrew Kings* (2nd ed.; Grand Rapids, 1965). The New Testament period chart is based on that in B. Metzger, *The New Testament Background, Growth and Content* (London, 1969), p.29.

The Documents

1 **'Temptation Seal'** First published in G. Smith, *The Chaldaean Account of Genesis* (London, 1875), pp. 90-91 with figure on p.91, and many times since. For standard publication with bibliography see D. Collon, *Catalogue of the Western Asiatic Seals in the British Museum. Cylinder Seals,* III, *Akkadian-Post Akkadian-Ur III Periods* (London, 1982), no. 302, p. 124, pl. XL.

2 **Ziggurat at Ur** The ziggurat at Ur in all its phases is described in C.L. Woolley, *Ur Excavations*, V, *The Ziggurat and its Surroundings* (London, 1939); ziggurats in general and their relevance to the Biblical account of the Tower of Babel are discussed in A. Parrot, *Ziggurats et tour de Babel* (Paris, 1949).

3 **Atrahasis Epic** Early translation of part of the Neo-Assyrian version in Smith, *Genesis* (no. 1), pp. 153–6 ['story of Atarpi']; an up to date edition is given in W.G. Lambert and A.R. Millard, *Atra-Hasis. The Babylonian Story of the Flood* (Oxford, 1969); and the relation to the Bible is discussed in Lambert, 'A New Look at the Babylonian Background of Genesis', *Journal of Theological Studies* 16 (1965), pp. 287–300; and Millard, 'A New Babylonian *Genesis* Story', *Tyndale Bulletin* 18 (1967), pp. 3–18; see also H. Schmokel in NERTROT, pp. 90–93. On the apparent absence of a flood account in third millennium sumer see M. Civil in Lambert and Millard, *Atrahasis*, p. 139, and on the Sumerian King List T. Jacobsen, *The Sumerian King List* (Chicago, 1939).

4 **Statue of Idri-mi** Text, translit., trans., and discussion in S. Smith, *The Statue of Idri-mi* (London, 1949); translation by A.L. Oppenheim in ANET, pp. 557–8. On the Hapiru see J. Bottero, *Le Problème des Habiru à la 4ᵉ Recontre Assyriologique Internationale* [Cahiers de la Société Asiatique, 13] (Paris, 1954); M. M. Greenberg, *The Hab/piru* [American Oriental Series, 39] (New Haven, 1955).

5 **Inscribed Sphinx** First published in W.M.F. Petrie, *Researches in Sinai* (London, 1906), fig. 141, and pp. 129–30; subsequently in A. Gardiner and T.E. Peet, *The Inscriptions of Sinai*, I (London, 1917), no. 345, p. 18, pl. LXXXII; recent discussion in W.F. Albright, *The Proto-Sinaitic Inscriptions and their Decipherment* [Harvard Theological Studies, XXII] (Cambridge, 1966), no. 345, p. 16, fig. 5.

6 **The Alphabet** On writing in general see I.J. Gelb, *A Study of Writing* (2nd ed.; Chicago, 1963); on the early phases of alphabetic writing J. Naveh, *The Early History of the Alphabet* (Jerusalem and Leiden, 1982); see also G.R. Driver, *Semitic Writing. From Pictograph to Alphabet* [Schweich Lectures, 1944] (3rd ed.; London, 1976). Convenient charts of the Phoenician, Hebrew and Aramaic scripts, filling gaps in the version offered here, are given in TSSI, 3, pp. 180–81; 1, pp. 117–18; and 2, pp. 187–8 respectively. On the digamma in Homer see J.L. Myres, *Homer and His Critics* (London,

1958), pp. 50–53. Ahiram Sarcophagus Inscription (column 4) in TSSI, 3, no. 4. Hermopolis Papyri (column 10) in TSSI, 2, no. 27. Qumran Script (column 11) in F.L. Cross, 'The Development of the Jewish Scripts', in G.E. Wright, *The Bible and the Ancient Near East* (London, 1961), fig. 2, line 4 (p. 138).

7   **Letter from Yapahu** Text in C. Bezold and E.A.W. Budge, *The Tell el-Amarna Tablets in The British Museum* (London, 1892), no. 49; translit. and trans. in J.A. Knudtzon, *Die El-Amarna Tafeln* [Vorderasiatische Bibliothek, 2] (Leipzig, 1907–1915), no. 299; trans in W.L. Moran, *Les lettres d'el-Amarna* [Litteratures anciennes du Proche-Orient, 13] (Paris, 1987), p. 529; and see Greenberg, *Hab/piru* (no. 6), pp. 49–50, no. 115; also IOTH, no. 2.

8   **Letter from Biridiya** Text in Bezold and Budge, *Amarna Tablets* (no. 7), no. 72; translit. and trans. in Kudtzon *Amarna Tafeln* (no. 7), no. 245; trans by W.F. Albright in ANET, p. 485; Moran *Lettres* (no. 7), pp. 470–71. The Canaanite glosses are listed by E. Ebeling in Knudtzon, *Amarna Tafeln*, II, pp. 1545–9, and under their alphabetic headings, and the designation 'Can.[aneen] Anc. [ien]', in C.F. Jean and J. Hoftijzer, *Dictionnaire des inscriptions Semitiques de l'ouest* (Leiden, 1965).

9   **The Capture of Joppa** Trans. by J.A. Wilson in ANET, pp. 22–3; E.F. Wente in W.K. Simpson (ed.), *The Literature of Ancient Egypt* (Yale University Press; New Haven and London, 1972), pp. 81–4. On *'pr* see Greenberg, *Hab/piru* (no. 4), pp. 56 and 161; and for other instances E. Edel in TGI, no. 12.

10   **Statue of Ramesses II** See T.G.H. James. *Ancient Egypt. An Introduction* (Rev. ed.; London, 1979), pl. 7 and p. 196.

11   **Brick of Ramesses II** See in general A.J. Spencer, *Brick Architecture in Ancient Egypt* (Warminster, 1979).

12   **Israel Stela** First publication in W.M.F. Petrie and W. Spiegelberg, *Six Temples at Thebes 1886.* (London, 1897), obverse (Amenhotep III), pp. 10–11, 23–6, pl. XI–XII, reverse (Merneptah), pp. 13, 26–8, pls. XIII–XIV; illustr. in M. Saleh and H. Sourouzian, *Official Catalogue. The Egyptian Museum. Cairo* (Munich-Mainz, 1987), no. 212; ANEP, nos. 342–3; trans. by J.A. Wilson in ANET, pp. 376–8; R.J. Williams in DOTT, pp. 137–41.

13   **Laver Stand** See H. Matthaus, *Metallgefässe und Gefässuntersatze der Bronzezeit, der geometrischen und archaischen Periode auf Cypern* [H. Muller-Karpe (ed.) Prahistorische Bronzefunde, II, 8] (Munich, 1985), no. 706, pp. 316–18, pls. 103, 104; for a discussion of 1 Kings 7:28–39 in the higher critical tradition see J. Skinner, *Kings* [The Century Bible] (London, 1904), pp. 127–135; see also T.C. Mitchell in J.E. Curtis (ed.) *Bronze-Working Centres of Western Asia c. 1000-539 BC* (London, 1988), p. 279.

14   **Inscribed Arrowhead** Text and illustra., with discussion of other inscribed arrowheads, in T.C. Mitchell, 'Another Phoenician Inscribed Arrowhead' in J.N. Tubb (ed.), *Palestine in the Bronze and Iron Ages. Papers in Honour of Olga Tufnell* (London, 1985), pp. 136–53.

15   **Kurkh Stela of Shalmaneser III** Text in CIWA, III, pls, 7–8; translit. and trans. in H. Genge, *Stelen neuassyrischen Könige* (Freiburg, 1965), pp. 9–10, 81–103, 154–5, 229–51, 295; trans. of extracts by A.L. Oppenheim in ANET, pp. 277–9; R. Borger in TGI, no. 19; and in TUAT, I.4 (1984), pp. 360–62; further details in W. Schramm, *Einleitung in die assyrischen Königsinschriften*, II, *934-722, BC* (Leiden, 1973), pp. 70–72; C.J. Gadd, *The Stones of Assyria* (London, 1936), p. 148; illustr. in S. Smith, *Assyrian Sculptures in the British Museum from Shalmaneser III to Sennacherib* (London, 1938), pl. I and see p. 5; see also IOTH, no. 16.

16   **Black Obelisk of Shalmaneser III** Illustr. with text in A.H. Layard, *Monuments of Nineveh* I (London, 1849), pls. 53–6; text in Layard, *Inscriptions in the Cuneiform Character from Assyrian Monuments* (London, 1851), pls. 87–98; translit. and trans. in E. Michel, *Welt des Orients* 2 (1954–9), pp. 137–57; 221–33; trans. of selections by A.L. Oppenheim in ANET, pp. 278–81; D.J. Wiseman in DOTT, p. 48; R. Borger in TUAT, I.4 (1984), pp. 362–3; further details in Schramm, *Einleitung* (no. 15), p. 79; Gadd, *Stones*, pp. 147–8; see also IOTH, no. 12. On ša *mātu imērišu* for 'Damascus' which also occurs as *mātu ša imērišu* and in other variant writings, literally

'(land) of his ass' or something of the kind, a designation perhaps not fully understood by the Assyrian scribes, see Oppenheim in ANET, p. 278, no. 8, and CAD, I/J, p 115.

17   **Deity in Fish Robe** Illustr. in Layard, *Monuments of Nineveh* II (London, 1853), pl. 6 and p. 2; see also Layard, *Discoveries in the Ruins of Nineveh and Babylon* (London, 1853), pp. 343, 350; Gadd, *Stones* (no. 15), p. 139; on 1 Sam. 5:4 see P.K. McCarter, *I Samuel* [Anchor Bible, 8] (Garden City, New York, 1980), pp. 119, 121–2.

18   **Moabite Stone** Illustr. in ANEP, no. 274; good copy of text in M. Lidzbarski, *Handbuch Der Nordsemitischen Epigraphik* II (Weimar, 1898), pl. I; translit. and trans. in KAI, no. 181; TSSI, I, pp. 71–83; trans. by W.F. Albright in ANET, pp. 320–21; E. Ullendorff in DOTT, pp. 195–8, pl. 10; K. Galling in TGI, no. 21; H-P Muller in TUAT, I.6 (1985), pp. 646–50; E. Lipinski in NERTROT, pp. 237–40; account of discovery in N.A. Silberman, *Digging for God and Country* (New York, 1982), pp. 100–112.

19   **Astartu Relief** See R.D. Barnett and M Falkner, *The Sculptures of Tiglath-pileser III (745-727 BC)* (London, 1962), p. 30 and pls. LXVIII–LXXI; Gadd, *Stones* (no. 15), p. 157; see also IOTH, no. 13.

20   **Sargon Relief** See Smith, *Assyrian Sculptures* (no. 15), pl. XXV, and p. 13; Gadd, *Stones* (no. 15), p. 161; P. Albenda, *The Palace of Sargon King of Assyria* (Paris, 1986), p. 167, fig. 61; see also IOTH, no. 14.

21   **Samaria Ivories** These fragments are part of the group published in J.W. and G.M. Crowfoot, *Early Ivories from Samaria* (London, 1938); selection in ANEP, nos. 129–30; see also R.D. Barnett, *Ancient Ivories in the Middle East and Ajacent Countries* [Qedem, 14] (Jerusalem, 1982), p. 49; see also IOTH, no. 9; and T.C. Mitchell, CAH, III, I. pp. 471, 506–7.

22   **Stamped Jar Handles** General study in P. Welten, *Die Königs-Stempel: Ein Beitrag zur Militärpolitik Judas unter Hiskia und Josia* (Wiesbaden, 1969); for identification of *mmšt* as Emmaus see A. Lemaire, *Revue Biblique,* 82 (1975), pp. 15–23.

23   **Assyrian Tribute List** Text in R.F. Harper, *Assyrian and Babylonian Letters* (London and Chicago, 1892–1914), VI, no. 632; translit. and trans. in R.H. Pfeiffer, *State Letters of Assyria* [American Oriental Series, 6] (New Haven, 1935), no. 96; J.N. Postgate, *Taxation and Conscription in the Assyrian Empire* [Studia Pohl. ser.mai., 3] (Rome, 1974), pp. 152–3; trans. in L. Waterman, *Royal Correspondence of the Assyrian Empire* (Ann Arbor, 1930–36), no. 632, A.L. Oppenheim in ANET, p. 301; see also IOTH, no. 15.

24   **Assyrian Scale Armour** R.D. Barnett in *British Museum Quarterly* 26 (1962–3), p. 95; see also on scale armour in general R.M. Boehmer, *Die Kleinfunde von Bogazkoy* [Wissenschaftliche Veröffentlichung der Deutschen Orient-Gesellschaft, 87] (Berlin, 1969), pp. 102–4; on *šuqšu* see E.A. Speiser, *Journal of the American Oriental Society* (1950), pp. 47–8; see also Mitchell in Curtis, *Bronze-Working* (no. 13), pp. 274–5.

25   **Royal Steward Inscription** First published (with tentative reference to Shebnah) in C. Clermont Ganneau, *Archaeological Researches in Palestine During the Years 1873-4,* I, (London, 1899), pp. 305–13; first effective decipherment in N. Avigad, 'The Epitaph of a Royal Steward from Siloam Village', IEJ 3 (1953), pp. 137–152; translit. and trans. in KAI, no. 191; TSSI. I, pp. 25–6; see also IOTH, no. 18.

26   **Annals of Sennacherib** Text in CIWA, I, pls. 37–42; translit. of account of third campaign in R. Borger, *Babylonisch-assyrische Lesestucke* (Rome, 1963), pp. 67–9; trans. by A.L. Oppenheim in ANET, pp. 287–8; D.J. Wiseman in DOTT, pp. 64–9; see also IOTH, no. 15. On Colonel R. (not J.G.) Taylor see E. Sollberger in *Anatolian Studies* 22 (1972), p. 129 and no. 3.

27   **Siege of Lachish Reliefs** Reliefs in Layard, *Monuments*, II (no. 17), pls. 20–24; A. Paterson, *The Palace of Sinacherib* (The Hague, 1915), pls. 68–76; parts in ANEP, nos. 371–4; translit. and trans. of text in D.D. Luckenbill, *The Annals of Sennacherib* [Oriental Institute Publications 2] (Chicago, 1924), p. 56, no. XXV; trans. by A.L. Oppenheim in ANET, p. 288; D.J. Wiseman in DOTT, pp. 69–70; see also IOTH, no. 17.

28   Vassal Treaty of Esarhaddon Text, translit. and trans. in D.J. Wiseman, 'The Vassal Treaties of Esarhaddon' *Iraq* 20 (1958); trans. by E. Reiner in ANET, pp. 534–41; see also H. Schmokel in NERTROT, pp. 129–31; for discussion of the relations between treaties and Biblical Covenants see D.J. McCarthy, *Treaty and Covenant* [Anlecta Biblica, 21] (Rome, 1963); K.A. Kitchen, *Ancient Orient and Old Testament* (London and Chicago, 1966), pp. 90–120, and in J.B. Payne, *New Perspectives on the Old Testament* (Waco, Texas and London, 1970), pp. 3–4.

29   Assyrian Eponym List Not yet identified by G. Smith, for his *Assyrian Eponym Canon* (1875, see p. 10 above); first published by C. Bezold in PSBA II (1889), pl. IIIb (text), pp. 286–7, no. 3; translit. and trans. in A. Ungnad 'Eponymen' in E. Ebling and B. Meissner (eds.), *Reallexikon der Assyriologie* II (Berlin and Leipzig, 1933–8), p. 434, Eponymenkanon C^b5. On *turtānu* see B. Meissner and W. von Soden, *Akkadische Handworterbuch* (Wiesbaden), p. 1332 (under *ta/urtānu*), and on *rab-šaqê* ibid., p. 940 (under *šaqu(m)*, 7).

30   Bilingual Clay Docket Text, translit. and trans. in J.H. Stevenson, *Assyrian and Babylonian Contracts with Aramaic Reference Notes* (New York, 1902), no. 2; CIS, II, no. 38; translit. and trans. of the Aramaic text in L. Delaporte, *Épigraphes araméens* (Paris, 1912), no. 21. On *rab ša rēši* see J.A. Brinkman, *A Political History of Post-Kassite Babylonia 1158-722 BC* [Analecta Orientalia, 43] (Rome, 1968), pp. 309–11; A.L. Oppenheim in *Journal of the Ancient Near East Society* 5 (1973), pp. 325–34.

31   Clay Tablet K.6205 (right hand fragment), ascribed to Tiglath-pileser III, first published in CIWA III, pl. IX.2 and incorporated in R. Rost, *Die Keilschrifttexte Tiglat-Pilesers III* (Leipzig, 1893), II, pl. XX, I, pp. 18–21 (lines 103–119); 82–3–23, 131 (left hand two fragments), ascribed to Sargon, first published in B. Meissner, *Orientalistische Literaturzeitung* 22 (1919), p. 113; H. Tadmor, 'The Campaigns of Sargon II of Assur: a Chronological-Historical Study', *Journal of Cuneiform Studies* 12 (1958), pp. 12–14; joining of the two tablets (recognised by Tadmor) and new interpretation in Naaman, 'Sennacherib's Letter to God', BASOR, 214 (1974), pp. 25–39; see also Borger, *Lesestücke* (no. 26), pp. 134–5.

32   Creation Epic First trans. in Smith, *Genesis* (no. 1), pp. 61–100; text in A. Deimel, *Enuma eliš^ sive epose babylonicum de creatione mundi* (2nd ed.; Rome, 1936; W.G. Lambert, *Enuma eliš. The Babylonian Epic of Creation* (Oxford, 1966); translit. and trans. in R. Labat, *Le poème babylonien de la création (Enūma eliš)* (Paris, 1935); trans. by E.A. Speiser in ANET, 60–72, (and A.K. Grayson, pp. 501–503); J.V. Kinnier-Wilson in DOTT, pp. 3–16 (selections); H. Schmökel in NERTROT, pp. 80–4 (selections); trans. with discussion of relation to the Old Testament in A. Heidel, *The Babylonian Genesis, The Story of Creation* (2nd ed.; Chicago, 1951).

33   Gilgamesh Epic First translation of Tablet XI in Smith, *Genesis* (no. 1), pp. 167–70, 172, 263–83 [Gilgamesh read as Izdubar]: text and translit. in R. Campbell Thompson, *The Epic of Gilgamesh* (Oxford, 1930); trans. by E.A. Speiser in ANET, pp. 93–6; Kinnier Wilson in DOTT, pp. 20–4; Schmökel in NERTROT, pp. 93–7; trans. with discussion in A. Heidel, *The Gilgamesh Epic and Old Testament Parallels* (2nd ed.; Chicago, 1949).

34   Moabite Seal First published by Sir Leonard Woolley, *Ur Excavations, IX, The Neo-Babylonian and Persian Periods* (London and Philadelphia, 1962), p. 32, 109 wrongly quoted as U.526; recognized by J.C. Greenfield and republished by N. Avigad in J.A. Saunders (ed.), *Near Eastern Archaeology in the Twentieth Century. Essays in Honor of Nelson Glueck* (Garden City, New York, 1970), p. 290, pl. 30.6.

35   Philistine Seal First published by H.C. Rawlinson in JRAS, New Series, 1 (1865), pp. 237–8, no. IX, pl. following p. 228; see later D. Diringer, *Le inscrizioni antico-ebraiche palestinesi* (Florence, 1934), pp. 233–4, no. 73, pl. XXI. 10; A. Bergman (later Biran) in *Journal of Biblical Literature* 55 (1936), pp. 224–6; H. Tadmor in *The Biblical Archaeologist* 29 (1966), pp. 98, fig. 12.

36   Iron Age Tomb Group Presented in 1865 by the Reverend Joseph Barclay who was later the Anglican Bishop of Jerusalem 1879–81, on whom see, briefly, M. Hannam in *Palestine Exploration Quarterly* 114 (1982), p. 63; published in J.N. Tubb, *An Iron Age II Tomb Group from the Bethlehem Region* [BMOP, 14] (London, 1980).

37   Paym Weight See D. Diringer in O. Tufnell, *Lachish III, The Iron Age* (London, 1953), pp. 315, 354, no. 37, pl. 51.9; in general Diringer in DOTT, pp. 229–30; on vocalisation as *paym*, Gibson, TSSI. I, p. 70, no. 10; on 1 Sam. 13:19–21 P.K. McCarter, *I Samuel* (no. 17) p. 238; on *pĕṣîrâ* G.R. Driver in *Archiv fur Orientforschung* 15 (1945-5), p. 68.

38   Beqa' Weight See Diringer in Tufnell, *Lachish III* (no. 37), pp. 351, 354 no. 40, pl. 51.13; in general Diringer in DOTT, p. 229; TSSI.I, p. 70 and no. 12.

39   Clay Sealing See N. Avigad in IEJ, 14 (1964), pp. 193–4, pl. 44c.

40   Brick of Nebuchadnezzar Translit. of cuneiform text with bibliography in C.B.F. Walker, *Cuneiform Brick Inscriptions in the British Museum* (London, 1981), no. 101; translit. and trans. in S. Langdon *Die neubabylonischen Königsinschriften* [Vorderasiatische Bibliothek, 4] (Leipzig, 1912), pp. 202–03, no. 40; Aramaic text first published [as *zbnk*] by H.C. Rawlinson in JRAS, New Series 1 (1865), pp. 228–9, no. I, pl. following p. 228; then in CIS III, no. 55; on *za-bi-na-a'* see M.D. Coogan, *West Semitic Personal Names in the Murašu Documents* (Missoula, 1976), pp. 23, 72; also R. Borger in TUAT, I, 4, p. 418; and T.C. Mitchell, 'The Nebuchadnezzar Brick CIS.III.55', forthcoming.

41   Lachish Ostracon First publication, text, translit., trans. and notes, in H. Torczyner, *Lachish I, The Lachish Letters* (London, 1938), pp. 33–43, no. II; translit. and trans. in KAI, no. 192; TSSI, 1, pp. 37–8; D. Pardee, *Handbook of Ancient Hebrew Letters* (Chico, California, 1982), pp. 78–81; trans. by W.F. Albright in ANET, p. 322; A. Lemaire, *Inscriptions hebraiques, I. Les ostraca* (Paris, 1977), pp. 97–100; see also IOTH, no. 19.

42   Nabonidus Cylinder Text in CIWA, I, pl. 68.1; translit. and trans. in Langdon, *Neubabylonischen Königsinschriften* (no. 40), pp. 250–53, Nabonidus 5; see also R.P. Dougherty, *Nabonidus and Belshazzar* (New Haven, 1929), p. 94.

43   Babylonian Chronicle Text, translit. and trans. in D.J. Wiseman, *Chronicles of Chaldaean Kings (626-556 BC) in the British Museum* (London, 1956), pp. 66–75 pls XIV-XVI; translit. and trans. in A.K. Grayson, *Babylonian and Assyrian Chronicles* (Locust Valley, 1975), pp. 99–102; trans. by A.L. Oppenheim in ANET, pp. 563–564; Wiseman in DOTT, pp. 80–81; see also IOTH, section 20.

44   Cyrus Cylinder Text in CIWA, V, pl. 35; translit. and trans. in F.H. Weissbach, *Die Keilschriften der Achämeniden* [Vorderasiatische Bibliothek, 3] (Leipzig, 1911), pp. 2–9; P.R. Berger in *Z.A.* 64 (1974-5), pp. 192–203; trans. by A.L. Oppenheim in ANET, pp. 315–6; T. Fish in DOTT, pp. 92–4; see also IOTH, section 21.

45   Behistun Inscription First publications by H.C. Rawlinson in JRAS, 10 (1847), pp. 1–349 (Old Persian version); 14 (1851), pp. 1–32 (Babylonian version); stylised text, translit. and trans. of all three versions in L.W. King and R. Campbell-Thompson, *The Sculptures and Inscription of Darius the Great on the Rock of Behistun in Persia* (London, 1907); translit. and trans. of the three versions in Weissbach, *Keilschriften der Achämeniden* (no. 44), pp. 8–79; Old Persian translit. and trans. (with bibliography) in R.G. Kent, *Old Persian. Grammar. Texts. Lexicon* (2nd ed.; New Haven, 1953), pp. 107–08, 116–35; Babylonian translit. and trans. E.N. von Voigtlander, *The Bisitun Inscription of Darius the Great. Babylonian Version* [CII, I.II.1] (London, 1978); conflated trans. of the three versions in R. Borger and W. Hinz in TUAT, I, 4 (1984), pp. 419–450. For fragments of an Aramaic version from Elephantine, that confirms the correctness of the decipherment, see A. Cowley, *Aramaic Papyri of the Fifth Century BC* (Oxford, 1923), pp. 248–71; J.C. Greenfield and B. Porten, *The Bisitun Inscription of Darius the Great. Aramaic Version* [CII. IV. 1] (London, 1982). On the decipherment see A.J. Booth, *The Discovery and Decipherment of the Trilingual Cuneiform Inscriptions* (London, 1902); S.A. Pallis, *The Antiquity of Iraq. A. Handbook of Assyriology* (Copenhagen, 1956), pp. 94–187; C.H. Gordon, *Forgotten*

Scripts (Rev. ed.; New York, 1982), pp. 40–67; C.B.F. Walker, *Cuneiform* (London, 1987), pp. 48–52.

46   **Seal of Parshandata** Inscription published by H.C. Rawlinson in JRAS New Series, 1 (1986), pp. 238–9, no. X, pl. facing p. 228; CIS, II, no. 100.

47   **Rosetta Stone** Trans of Greek text in C. Andrews, *The Rosetta Stone* (London, 1981), pp. 25–8; U. Kaplony-Heckel in TUAT, 1, 3 (1983) pp. 236–46. On the decipherment see A. Gardiner, *Egyptian Grammar. Being an Introduction to the Study of Hieroglyphs* (3rd ed.; Oxford, 1957), pp. 12–16; Andrews, *Rosetta Stone*; W.V. Davies, *Egyptian Hieroglyphs* (London, 1987), pp. 47–56.

48   **Letter from Isias** Text and trans. in G. Milligan, *Selections from the Greek Papyri* (Cambridge, 1910), no. 4; A.S. Hunt and C.C. Edgar, *Select Papyri*, I, *Non-Literary Papyri and Private Affairs* [Loeb Classical Library, 226] (London and Cambridge, Mass., 1932), no. 97; trans in C.K. Barrett, *The New Testament Background: Selected Documents* (Rev. ed.; London, 1987), no. 21. On the bearing of papyrus discoveries on New Testament Greek see A. Deissmann, *Light from the Ancient East* (London, 1927; repr. Grand Rapids, 1965); A.T. Robertson, *A Grammar of the Greek New Testament in the Light of Historical Research* (4th ed.; London, 1923); J.H. Moulton and G. Milligan, *The Vocabulary of The Greek Testament Illustrated from the Papyri and Other Non-Literary Sources* (London 1930).

49   **Qumran Jar** For a survey and bibliography of Qumran studies see G. Vermes, *The Dead Sea Scrolls. Qumran in Perspective* (London, 1977), and for translations of the non-Biblical texts, Vermes, *The Dead Sea Scrolls in English* (3rd ed.; Harmondsworth, 1987); see also IOTH, no. 24.

50   **Head of Augustus** First published by J. Garstang in *Liverpool Annals of Archaeology and Anthropology* 4 (1912), p. 51; and R.C. Bosanquet in *ibid.*, pp. 66–71; see also S. Walker and A. Burnett, *Augustus. Handlist of the Exhibition and Supplementary Studies* [BMOP, 16] (London, 1981), no. 77. On Augustus in general see bibliography in M. Cary and H.H. Scullard, *A History of Rome Down to the Reign of Constantine* (3rd ed.; London, 1975), p. 628, no. 1.

51   **Bust of Tiberius** A.H. Smith, *A Catalogue of Sculpture in the Department of Greek and Roman Antiquities British Museum.* III (London, 1904), no. 1880. On Tiberius in general see Cary and Scullard, *History* (no. 50), p. 632, no. 1.

52   **Head of Claudius** Smith, *Catalogue* (no. 51), II (1900), no. 1155. On Claudius in general see Cary and Scullard, *History* (no. 50), p. 633, no. 14.

53   **Head of Nero** Smith, *Catalogue* (no. 51), III, no. 1887. On Nero in general see Cary and Scullard, *History* (no. 50), p. 634, no. 20.

54   **Papyrus Census Order** Text and trans. in Milligan, *Selections* (no. 48), no. 28; Hunt and Edgar, *Select Papyri* (no. 48), II, *Non Literary Papyri. Public Documents* [Loeb Class. Lib., 282] (1934), no. 220.

55   **Fragments of Unknown Gospel** Text and trans. in H.I. Bell and T.C. Skeat, *Fragments of an Unknown Gospel and other Early Christian Papyri* (London, 1935). pp. 1–41; trans. with discussion and bibl. by J. Jeremias in E. Hennecke (ed. by) W. Schneemelcher, *New Testament Apocrypha*, I, *Gospels and Related Writings* (London, 1963), pp. 94–7; see also F.F. Bruce, *Jesus and Christian Origins Outside The New Testament* (London, 1974), pp. 160–64. For Gospel dates see F.F. Bruce, *The New Testament Documents* (6th ed.; Leicester, 1982), p. 12.

56   **Politarch Inscription** Text in C.T. Newton, *The Collection of Ancient Greek Inscriptions in the British Museum*, II (Oxford 1883; repr. Milan, 1978), no. 171; text and trans. in B.F. Cook, *Greek Inscriptions* (London, 1987), pp. 22–3; see also E.D. Burton in *American Journal of Theology* 2 (1898), pp. 598–632; and Moulton and Milligan *Vocabulary of the Greek Testament* (no. 48), p. 525 under *politarchēs*.

57   **Coin of Ephesus** B.V. Head, *British Museum. Catalogue of the Greek Coins of Ionia* (London, 1892), p. 78, no. 234; see also W.F. Arndt and F.W. Gingrich, *A Greek-English Lexicon of the New Testament and Other Early Christian Literature* (2nd ed.; Chicago and London), p. 537 under *neōkoros*.

58   **Bronze Assarion** Head, *Catalogue* (no. 57), p. 343, no. 127.

59   **Codex Sinaiticus** Facsimile edition in H. and K. Lake, *Codex Sinaiticus Petropolitanus* 2 vols (Oxford, 1922 and 1911); see also F. Kenyon, *Our Bible and the Ancient Manuscripts* (5th ed. rev. by A.W. Adams; London, 1958), pp. 119–20, 191–8; K. and B. Aland, *The Text of the New Testament* (Grand Rapids and Leiden, 1987), pp.106–07; T.S. Pattie, *Manuscripts of the Bible* (British Library; London 1979), pp. 14–23; on the 'Textus Receptus' and Erasmus's extraordinary editorial method see Aland, *Text*, pp. 4–7; see also F.F. Bruce, *The Books and the Parchments* (2nd ed.; London, 1953), pp. 177–8.

60   **Hebrew Pentateuch** See C.D. Ginsburg, *Introduction to the Massoretico-Critical Edition of the Hebrew Bible* (London, 1897), pp. 469–74; E. Wurthwein, *The Text of the Old Testament, An Introduction to the Biblica Hebraica* (Grand Rapids, 1979), pp. 164–5.

Index of Biblical References

Luke

2:1	91
2:1–4	95
3:1	92
5:12–14	96
6:46	96
12:6	99
20:22	92
20:24, 25	92
20:20–23	96
23:2	92
23:38	30

John

3:2	96
5:2	30
10:25	96
18:31–33	96
18:37–38	96
19:12	92
19:13	30
19:15	92
19:17	30
19:20	30

Acts

3:19	89
7:22	88
11:28	93
15:23	89
17:6	98
17:7	93
17:8	98
18:2	93
19:29	98
19:24	99
19:27–28	99
19:29	98
19:34–35	99
20:4	98
21:40	30
22:2	30
23:26–30	89
25:21	94
26:14	30
28:19	94

Romans

1:1–7	89
16:21	98

2 Corinthians

11:22	30

1 Timothy

1:1–2	89

2 Timothy

1:1–2	89
1:16	89

Titus

1:1–4	89

James

1:1	89

Revelation

9:11	30
16:16	30

BRITISH MUSEUM

Western Asiatic

21946	43
48288–96	36
48502	35
78941	3
89152	46
89326	1
90136	40
90920	44
91032	26
91125	42
93091	36
102755	36
116598	34
118822	20
118884	15
118885	16
118908	19
124573	17
124902–15	27
125205	25
125702	41
130738	4
131444	49
131444A	49
132061	22
132065	22
132548	28
132699	24
132828	38
134695	39
136753	14
160142	22
160316	37
160317	22
E.29832	7
E.29855	8
K.1295	23
K.1689	42
K.3375	33
K.5419	32
K.6205	31
81–2–4,147	30
82–3–23,131	31
82–5–22,526	29
L.31–48	21

Egyptian

E.24	47
E.67	10
E.6020	11
E.10060	9
E.41748	5

Greek & Roman

GR.1805.7– 3.246	53
GR.1812.6–15.5	51
GR.1870.3–20.200	52
GR.1877.5–11.1	56
GR.1911.9– 1.1	50
GR.1946.10–17.1	13
GR. Sculpt.1206	57

Coins & Medals

BMC Chios 127	58
BMC Ephesus 234	57

BRITISH LIBRARY

Western Manuscripts

Add Ms 43725	59
Papyrus Egerton 2	55
Papyrus 42	48
Papyrus 904	54

Oriental Manuscripts

Or. 4445	60

PALESTINE EXPLORATION FUND

PEF.1–18	21

LOUVRE

5066	18

CAIRO MUSEUM

34025	12

General Index